Shuters Mathematics

Grade 8

Learners Book

J. Cross
S. Cross
G. Gull
S. Tonkin

Shuter & Shooter

PIETERMARITZBURG • CAPE TOWN • RANDBURG

Acknowledgements

The author team wishes to acknowledge the valuable contribution made by Mr. Archie Dlulisa of Shayabantu Secondary School in Sweetwaters, Pietermaritzburg, who read through, and commented on, the material produced by them.

IT IS ILLEGAL TO PHOTOCOPY ANY PAGES FROM THIS BOOK WITHOUT THE WRITTEN PERMISSION OF THE COPYRIGHT HOLDER

Shuter & Shooter Publishers (Pty) Ltd
Gray's Inn, 230 Church Street
Pietermaritzburg, South Africa 3201
://http.www.shuter.co.za

Copyright © Shuter & Shooter Publishers (Pty) Ltd 2000

All rights reserved.

No part of this publication may be
reproduced, stored in or introduced into a retrieval system,
or transmitted, in any form or by any means, electronic,
mechanical, photocopying, recording or otherwise, without the prior
written permission from the publisher.

Any person who commits any unauthorized act in relation to this publication may be liable to criminal prosecution and civil claims for damages.

First edition 2000
Seventh impression 2002

ISBN 0 7960 1507 4

Illustrations by Beverley de Meyer and Lynne de la Motte
Layout and design by AN dtp Services
Printed and bound by Interpak Books, Pietermaritzburg

Contents

1. Shapes 1
2. To vote or not to vote? 13
3. Making ends meet 22
4. Furnishing a flat 35
5. Who is top of the log? 46
6. What's cooking in the kitchen? 57
7. Finding our way with maps 64
8. Homes for all 75
9. A collection of containers 84
10. Running a car 92
11. Money, money, money 104
12. Planning a holiday 114
13. What is the chance? 123
14. Numeracy skills 134
15. Basic algebra 153

To the learner

Here are a few suggestions which, we hope, will help you as you work through this book.

- Unit 14 includes a number of exercises to test your numeracy skills. It may be useful to do this unit at the beginning of the year, to help you with your calculations at a later stage.

- As often as is possible, work together **in small groups**. If you are part of a very large class, work **in pairs** with the person closest to you. Working together will help you to share ideas and solve problems a little faster.

- Be prepared to take your Mathematics **outside the classroom** into the village, town or city in which you live. Mathematics is everywhere. This is why we call it Real Life Mathematics.

- Some of the problems in this book have **more than one correct answer**. This is where we ask you to think creatively, to come up with new and interesting ideas.

- We, the authors, have enjoyed putting together all the exercises and problems that you will find in this book. We sincerely hope that you will also get enjoyment and satisfaction out of using this book.

The authors

UNIT 1

Shapes

The diagram shows a painting on the wall of a Ndebele home. People from all over the world come to look at the beautiful artwork on these homes and in the beadwork of the Ndebele people. There is a lot of Mathematics in their art, shown by patterns of common mathematical shapes like triangles, rectangles, squares and many others. These patterns are often repeated on the walls of their houses. Look at the above illustration. Find as many different shapes as you can and write them down. Count the number of each of these shapes and write it down.

In this unit you will be given the opportunity to:
- look for different shapes in a diagram
- see how these shapes can form different interesting patterns
- measure angles to see the relationships between the angles in different shapes
- use these relationships to find unknown angles.

Activity 1: Dividing a village between 2 sons

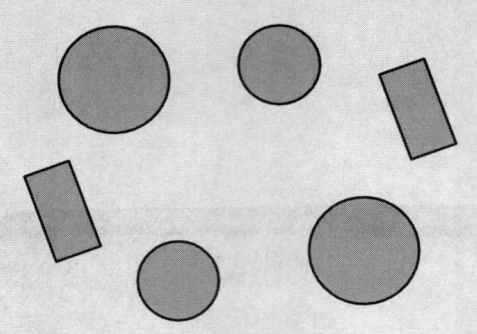

The above diagram represents a village as seen from above. You are the King of the village with twin sons. You want to divide the village into two equal parts so that your sons get the same inheritance. What is the fairest way to do this?
- Copy the diagram onto a piece of paper and try to fold the paper so that the fold divides the village equally. In how many ways can this be done?
- Can you add 2 more huts to the village plan and still divide it evenly? Where would you put them?
- Can you add 3 more huts and still divide it evenly? Where would you put them?

Let us do some more paper folding:

Take a piece of paper and fold it in half. Then tear out a shape at the fold. Now open the paper and see what you observe.

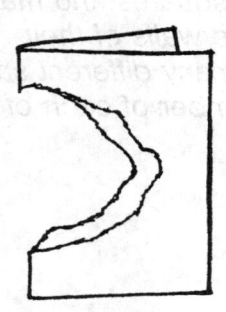

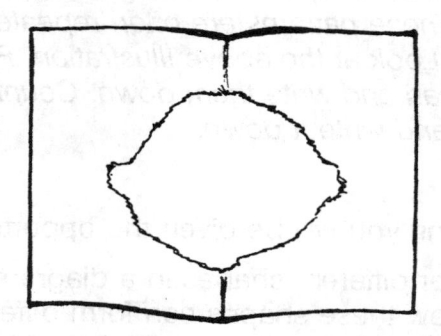

The shape is the same on either side of the fold. This fold is called the **axis of symmetry.**

Symmetry

A lot of shapes are pleasing to look at. This is sometimes due to a property called **symmetry**. Symmetry has different forms.

For example, the letter H is symmetrical.

A vertical line cuts it in half longways.

A horizontal line cuts it in half sideways.

This is called line **symmetry**. Each time the dotted line acts like a mirror, reflecting the one half onto the other. We say each part is a **mirror image** of the other. A line of symmetry is also called an axis of symmetry.

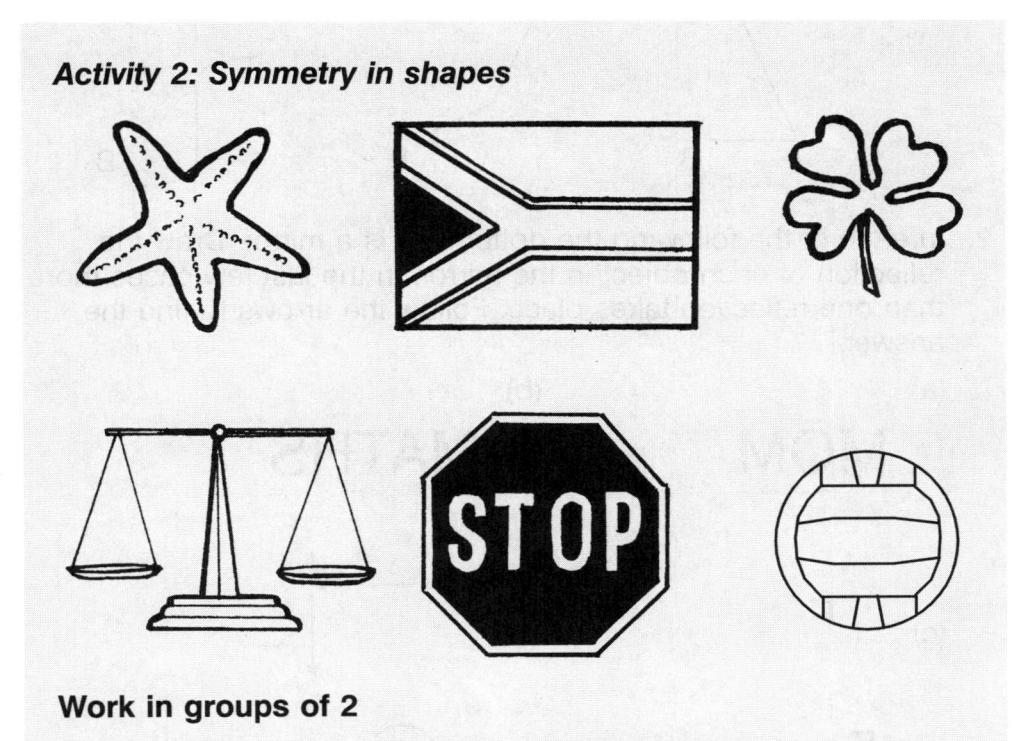

Activity 2: Symmetry in shapes

Work in groups of 2

All of the above diagrams have some sort of line symmetry. Discuss each diagram and refer to symmetry. Some diagrams may have to be slightly altered to make them have line symmetry. See how many lines of symmetry you can find in each diagram.

> **INVESTIGATE** ■□■□■□■□
>
> Choose one of the following topics to investigate:
> (a) Symmetry in nature, for example in trees, flowers etc
> (b) Symmetry in art such as paintings, pottery, baskets, jewellery, etc
>
> Present your findings on a poster. Show diagrams of the objects and explain where the symmetry is.

Exercise 1

1. In each of the diagrams, complete the drawings by putting in the mirror image. (In each case the dotted line AB is the axis of symmetry or mirror).

    (a)   (b) 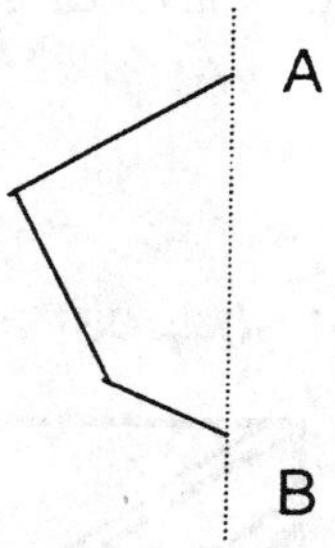   (c)

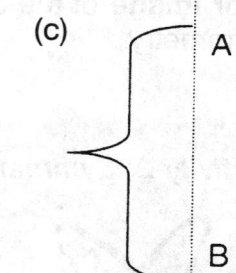

2. In each of the following the dotted line is a mirror. Draw the reflection of each object in the mirror. In the last few cases more than one reflection takes place. Follow the arrows to find the answer.

    (a) MOM

    (b) MATHS

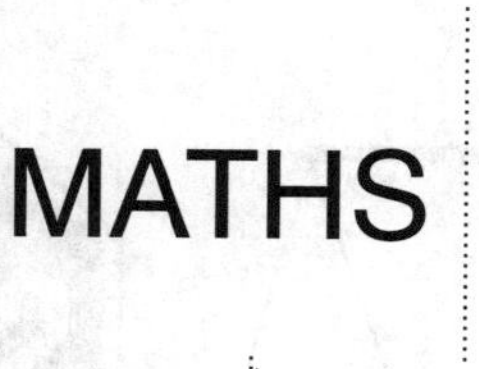

    (c) F

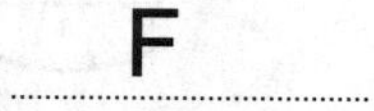

    (d) F →↓

    (e) 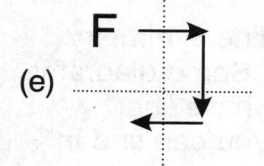 F →↓←

    (f)

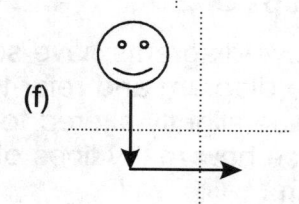

Quadrilaterals

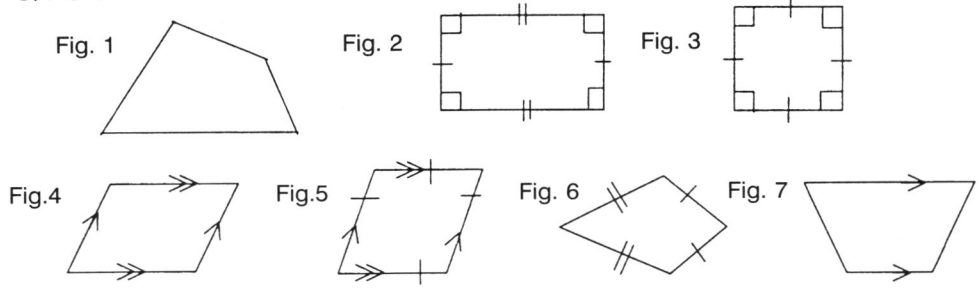

Fig. 1
Fig. 2
Fig. 3
Fig.4
Fig.5
Fig. 6
Fig. 7

Activity 3: Symmetry in quadrilaterals (4 sided figures)

Look at all the above quadrilaterals.

Have they got any lines of symmetry?

Complete the following table:

Figure	0 lines of symmetry	1 line of symmetry	2 lines of symmetry	3 lines of symmetry	4 lines of symmetry
1					
2					
3					
4					
5					
6					
7					

Use the definitions below to match the names to the 7 diagrams above.
- Quadrilateral: any four-sided figure
- Rectangle: a special quadrilateral with opposite sides equal and each angle 90°.
- Square: a special rectangle with all sides equal.
- Parallelogram: a special quadrilateral whose opposite sides are parallel.
- Rhombus: a special parallelogram with all of its sides equal.
- Kite: a special quadrilateral with two pairs of sides next to each other equal.
- Trapezium: a special quadrilateral with one pair of opposite sides parallel.

A polygon is a figure with many sides. A pentagon is a figure with 5 sides (pent means 5) and a hexagon is a figure with 6 sides (hex means 6). How many lines of symmetry does the hexagon alongside have?

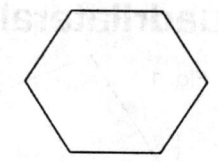

Measuring angles

Angles are measured using a protractor. A protractor is made of plastic and has two scales marked from 0° to 180°. One scale begins on the left and the other begins on the right. You place the centre of the protractor on the vertex of the angle and one side along the 0° line. The other side then gives the size of the angle. If the arms of the angle are not long enough to measure with the protractor, extend them using a ruler.

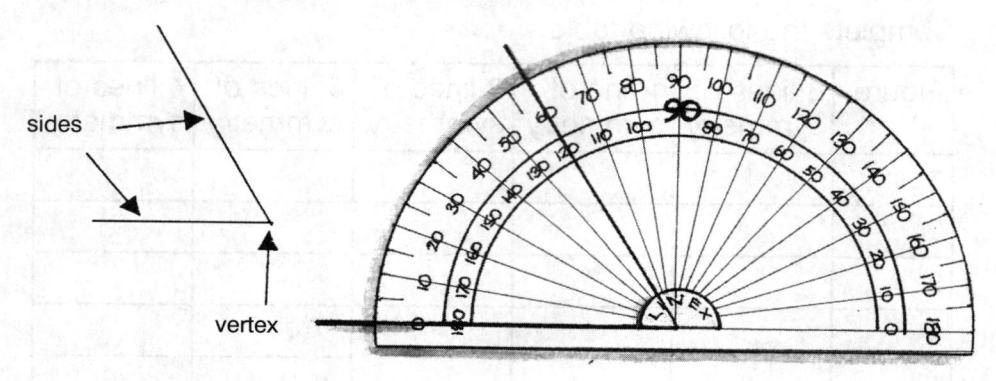

This would be an angle of 60°.

Exercise 2

1. Estimate the size of each of the following angles:

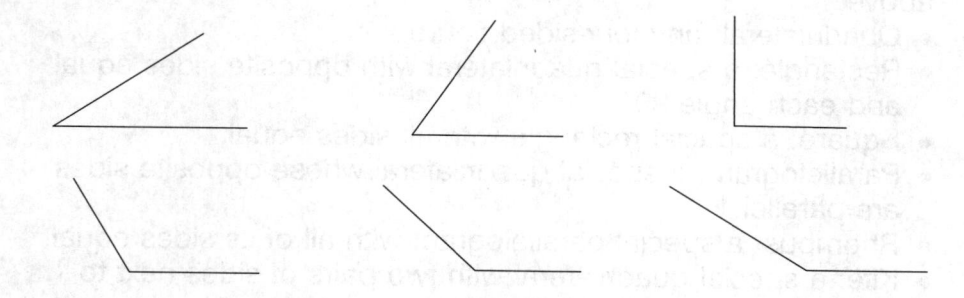

2. Now put your protractor over each diagram and measure them to see how well you guessed.

Tessellations (or tiling)

Tessellations are formed when we cover a particular surface area with various shapes, without leaving any gaps or having any of the shapes overlapping.

There are many examples of tessellations, for example a wall or floor that is tiled, or brick paving. A good example of a tessellation is the honeycomb in a beehive.

Here we cover a surface area with one shape only, the hexagon.

Look at the following tessellation of 6 bricks on a wall. The bricks are of rectangular shape where the length of each brick is twice the breadth:

This can also be arranged as:

PROBLEM SOLVER

Try and arrange the following 8 bricks in as many different ways as you can and still only cover the same area. You can copy the dotted grid on the right into your notebook and use that to tile the same size area:

Activity 4: Colouring in shapes

The diagram below is a tessellation using different shapes.

Photocopy the diagram and then colour in the diagram using four different colours. See how many shapes and patterns you can make.

Activity 5: Looking for shapes

In groups of 2, discuss any symmetry in the diagram.

Fencing

Different types of fences have different patterns.

A fence looks like this:

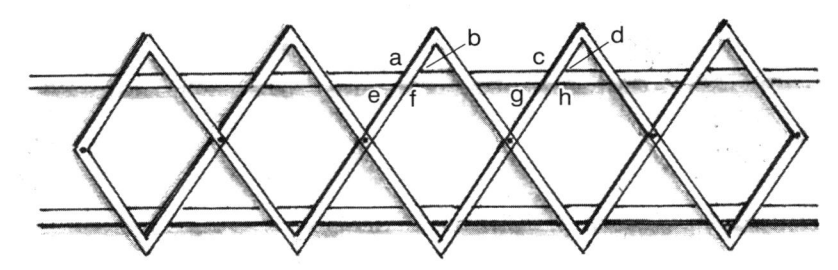

Exercise 3

Take a protractor and carefully measure the angles marked a, b, c, ... etc.

1. What do you notice about a and f; e and b; c and h; g and d?
2. What do you notice about b and g; f and c?
3. What do you notice about b and c; f and g?
4. What do you notice about a and b; e and f; c and d; g and h?

The diagram below is a farm gate:

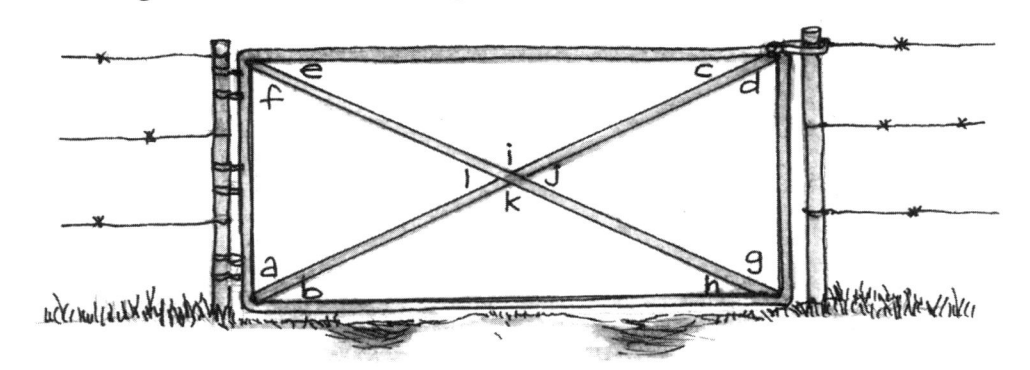

Exercise 4

Take a protractor and measure the angles marked a, b, c, ... etc.

1. What do you notice about a and d; b and c; e and h; f and g?
2. What do you notice about a, b, e and f?
3. What do you notice about c, d, g and h?
4. How many triangles are there in the diagram?
5. What is the sum of the angles of each triangle?
6. How many lines of symmetry does the diagram have?

Exercise 5

Write down the answers to the following (do not measure the angles, but look for relationships by looking at the fence diagrams):

1. AB is parallel to CD.
   This is written as AB || CD.
   Find a, b, c, and d in that order.

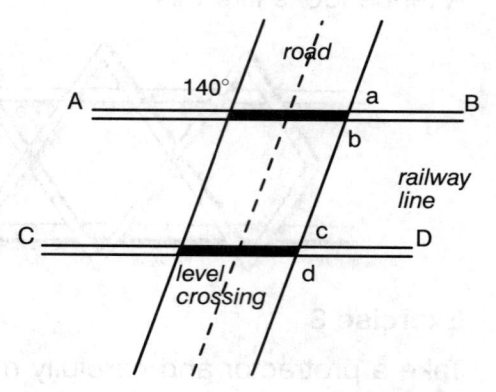

2. Find x, y and z in the two diagrams below

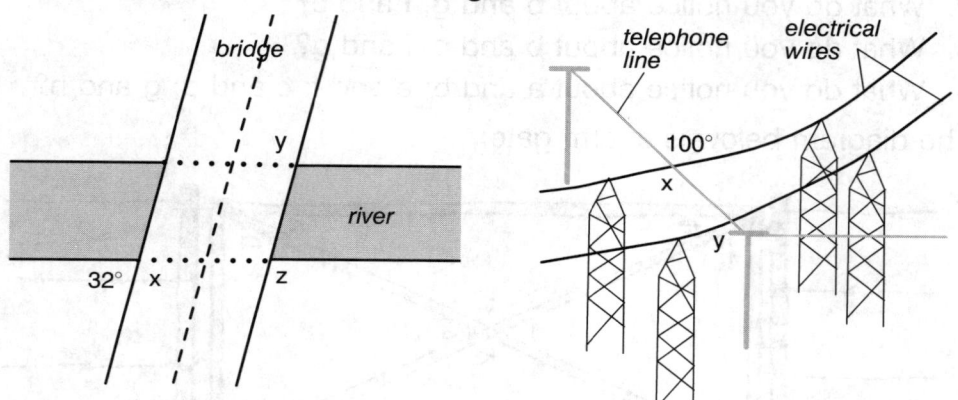

From the above diagrams you should have noticed that:

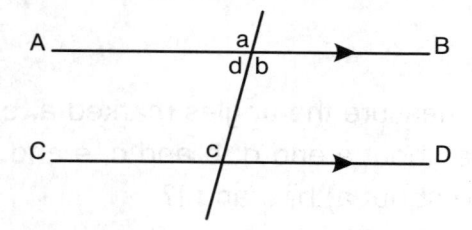

If AB || CD then a = c. a and c are called corresponding angles.
If AB || CD then b = c. b and c are called alternate angles.
If AB || CD then c + d = 180. c and d are called co-interior angles.

3. Find x and y

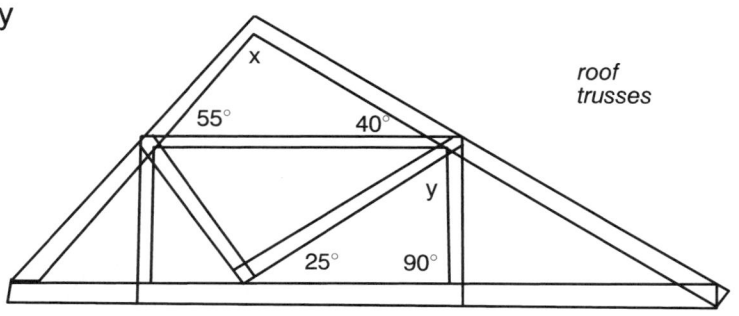

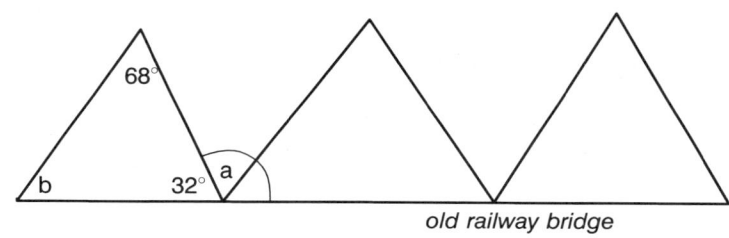

roof trusses

4. a = ...
   b = ...
   Notice:
   a = b + ...

old railway bridge

5. Find z:

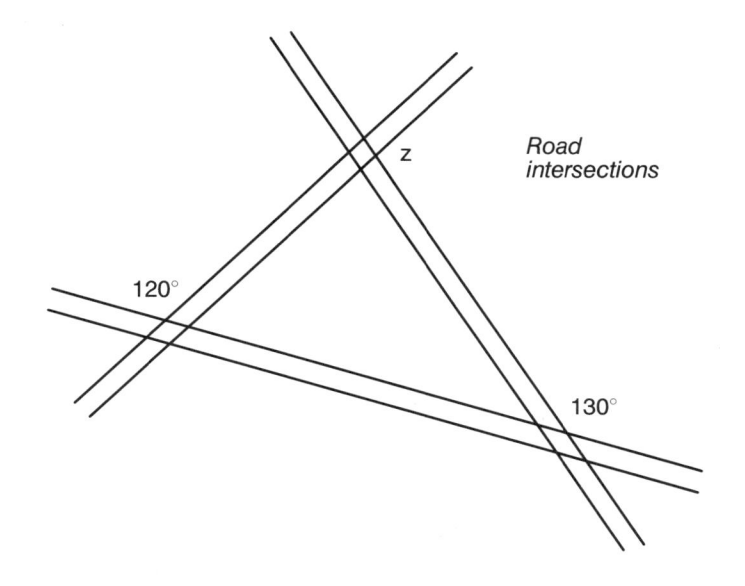

Road intersections

6. Find d, e and f

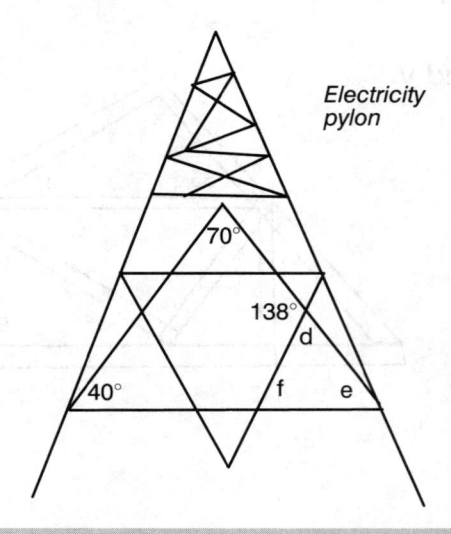

Electricity pylon

PROBLEM SOLVER

Using the fact that the sum of the angles of a triangle is 180°, try and work out the sum of the angles of the following figures:

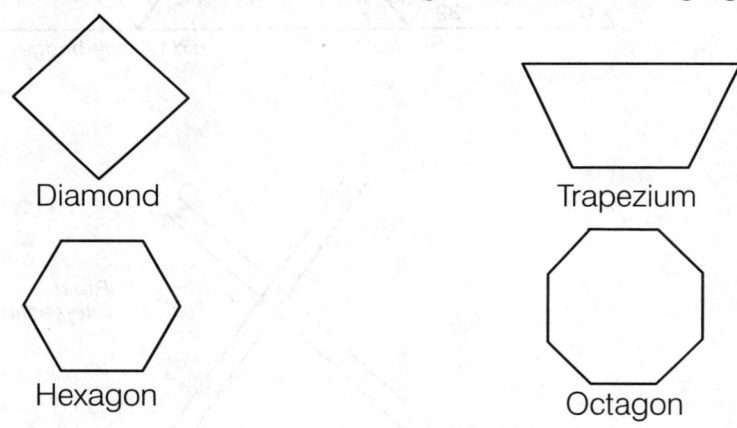

Diamond

Trapezium

Hexagon

Octagon

How did you do?

- Were you able to do a chart on symmetry in nature, buildings or art?
- Could you see the corresponding and alternate angles in the fence diagram? If not, try exercise 3 again.
- Were you able to complete exercises 4 and 5 on triangles successfully? If not, look at the farm gate example again.
- Which part of this unit did you find the most interesting? Why?
- Which part did you struggle with? Did you solve your problems?

UNIT 2

To Vote Or Not To Vote

The decade of the nineties has seen many dramatic changes in the history of our country. The picture above shows one of these. Who is our second president in the new South Africa? How did he come to be president? Why is South Africa different from many other African countries? Before the last election there was a lot of talk about who would be in the majority in the provinces, particularly KwaZulu-Natal. Some organisations tried to predict the results of the election by speaking to people in the provinces and asking them who they would vote for. This data, or information, was often seen in the newspapers. These organisations had to decide which people to ask, what questions they would ask the people, and how they would show this information to the rest of the population.

In this unit you will be given the opportunity to:
- decide if something is worth investigating
- look at results and see how they sometimes differ from what is expected
- use a tally table
- decide on the size of a sample
- collect data
- read a table.

Activity 1: Is it worth investigating?

Women in business · Causes of road accidents · Drugs in sport

Fashion trends · Different foods favoured by different cultures · Money earned by people in different professions

In pairs, discuss the above topics, and decide whether there is any use in collecting more data about them. Choose one that you think would be the most interesting and necessary, and report back to the class why you have chosen that topic.

Questions you could ask yourselves are:
- Who would this investigation help?
- What would it be used for?
- Is this a valuable topic from the point of view of politics, culture, economics (can someone make money out of knowing the answer to some questions on this topic)?
- Can it help socially (can some people's lives be made easier as a result of this survey)?

Think of some other topics that you think might be worth collecting data about.

How democracy works

In a democratic country, everyone over a certain age (usually 18) is allowed to vote in the country's elections to show who, or which political party, they would like to be in charge in the government. The data that we would be looking at in this situation, is the vote of each person in the country. How is this vote found out? The country has a General Election, where each person who qualifies to vote is allowed to go on the Election Day to cast their vote (put their choice in a ballot box). These votes are then sent to a counting station, where the number of votes for each party in each region (or area) is counted. The party with the most votes in each province is allowed to form the government for that province.

Activity 2: Using a tally table to count votes.

Each time a vote for a certain party comes up, a line is put in the correct column. After 4 lines the group is crossed out, which then represents 5 votes. Complete the following table:

Party	Votes counted	No. of votes
ACDP	||	2
ANC	|	
AZAPO	|	
DP		
NNP	||	7
FF	|	
IFP		
MF	|	
PAC	|	
UDM	|||	

Opinion polls

Before each General Election there is a lot of information that is collected to try to predict (guess) which party will be the majority (get the most votes) in the new government. The following shows the opinion polls for the Provincial government of KwaZulu-Natal at certain times before the 1999 General Election. All numbers are percentages:

	Sept-Oct 1994	Sept-Nov 1995	June-July 1997	Sept 1998	Oct-Nov 1998	Feb-Mar 1999	Actual provincial results
ANC	46	36	34	28	29	38	40
IFP	16	16	23	23	25	20	42
NNP	7	10	7	11	7	8	3
DP	1	3	3	6	3	5	8
UDM	0		3	1	2	1	1
MF			1	1	1	2	3
ACDP	<1	<1	1	1	1	<1	2
PAC	1	1	1	1	<1	<1	<1
FF	2	4	1	2	1	1	<1

Exercise 1

1. Look at the row labelled ANC. What percentage of the vote did the ANC expect to get in KwaZulu-Natal just before the election? Had they always expected to get this? What did they actually get?
2. Look at the row labelled IFP. Answer the same questions as you did for the ANC.
3. Which party do you think surprised the public the most with its election results? Why?
4. Which party do you think was the least surprised with their result?
5. Which party do you think was the most disappointed? Why?
6. Which party do you think was the happiest? Why?
7. Why do you think the results were not the same as expected?
8. Before the election was held, how do you think the data for the opinion polls was gathered?
9. What is the use of gathering data like this before an election?

Activity 3: Selecting a Students Representative Council (SRC)

You are to select 2 class representatives from 5 people who have been nominated.

1. Nominate 5 people in your class to stand for the position of SRC representative. The people nominating and seconding the nomination (the nominators) must each give a 3 to 5 minute speech on why they have nominated that person. The person nominated (the nominee) must also give a 3 to 5 minute talk on why he/she should be chosen as the SRC representative.

2. Now select 2 people to act as newspaper reporters and go to each person in the class to find out the opinion of the class.

3. The reporters should display their results on a table for the class to see.

4. The class should then vote privately using a sealed box.

5. A team of counters must then count the votes. Decide amongst yourselves how the counters should be selected. Complete a tally table to decide who the SRC representative for the class is.

6. As a standard: Do the same thing, but now find an SRC representative for the whole standard.

7. As a Junior Secondary Section: Do the same thing, but now find an SRC representative for the whole of Grade 8 and 9 together.

8. In your classes:
   Display your tally tables for the whole class.
   What do you notice about the results?
   Are some of the same people selected for all three groups? If not, why do you think this is so?

INVESTIGATE ■□■□■□■□■□

- You are going to collect data about the type of transport that is used by pupils in your school to get to school.
- Use a tally table to collect your data.
- Use the categories: taxi; bus; private car; foot; bicycle; motorbike (add others if you need to)
- Start by collecting data from your class.
- Display your results in a table.
- Next use the whole grade as your sample.
- Again display your results in a table.
- Lastly use the whole school as your sample.
- Again display your results in a table.

For discussion: What is the use of doing this three times, using a bigger sample each time?

Activity 4: How old are Grade 8 learners?

Find out how many learners in Grade 8 are 11 years old, 12 years old, 13 years old, 14 years old and so on, until you have covered all the ages in your grade.

Use a tally table to collect your data and then display your data in a table.

Stem and leaf diagrams

A stem and leaf diagram is very useful when you are trying to collect data which involves numbers. It can also be used to sort numbers into different orders.

Below are the results of a grade 8 Maths test. All the marks are percentages (out of 100).

56	67	87	56	55	64	62	69	76	77
63	67	91	65	68	59	58	90	87	71
53	55	62	69	71	35	66	72	78	45

If I want to find out how many people got marks in the sixties or seventies, it could be quite difficult by just looking at this list. If I rewrite the marks in a stem and leaf diagram, it is easier to see at a glance how many people achieved a certain mark.

The numbers that stand for the tens are written down as the *stem,* and the units are written down as the *leaves.*

For 56 I write a 6 next to the **5**

For 67 I write a 7 next to the **6**

For 87 I write a 7 next to the **8**

For 56 I write another 6 next to the **5**

For 55 I write a 5 next to the **5**

```
              1
              2
              3
              4
    stem      5      6, 6, 5
              6      7              leaf
              7
              8      7
              9
```

Use the marks above to complete this stem and leaf diagram.

We can rewrite the stem and leaf diagram so that you can see the marks in numerical order.

For example the row of the fifties should look like this:

    5   6, 6, 5, 9, 8, 3, 5

To write it in order from lowest to highest would mean I rewrite it as:

    5   3, 5, 5, 6, 6, 8, 9

Rewrite the above diagram so that you can read the marks in ascending order (from smallest to biggest)

Another use of a stem and leaf diagram is to show results that are separated in two different categories. In this case: marks of boys and marks of girls.

The marks below show the term results for the boys and girls in your grade.

Girls				Boys			
56	67	74	66	78	34	91	55
54	31	55	45	71	54	64	55
51	43	87	65	44	42	53	62
69	76	88	34	41	53	51	65
56	57	81	89	46	65	68	69

We can use a double stem and leaf diagram to show these marks. I have done the first line for you. You complete it.

Girls		Boys
	1	
	2	
	3	4
	4	
6	5	5
6,7	6	
4	7	8
	8	
	9	1

PROBLEM SOLVER

The following teams played in a tournament.

Work out how many games were played and the results of each game.

Team	Games played	Won	Drawn	Lost	Goals For	Goals Against
Chiefs	3	2	1	0	4	0
Swallows	3	2	0	1	3	3
Bushbucks	3	1	0	2	4	4
Amazulu	3	0	1	2	0	4

How did you do?

- Could you complete the tally table of election votes and then use a tally table in the investigations?
- Did you understand how to do the stem and leaf plot? If not, read the explanation on page 19 again.
- Did you discuss how to decide on the size of the sample that you use to collect data? Did increasing the size of the sample in the investigation make any difference to your data?
- Which part of this unit did you find the most enjoyable?
- Which part of this unit was the most interesting for you?

UNIT 3

Making ends Meet

We cannot just go out and buy things that we want, but we all know the feeling of wanting to do so. We have to think carefully about how to spend our money. We need to think about those things on which we have to spend money (like food and housing) and those things on which we would like to spend money (like sweets and magazines). We can think of these things as needs and wants (or necessities and luxuries). We also have to know the cost of things before we can decide how to spend our money. This all needs careful planning!

Do you know what is meant by 'making ends meet'?
Give examples of luxuries and necessities.
Compare your examples with those of others.

In this unit, you will:
- plan how to spend your own money
- think of ways to make your money go further
- think of ways of earning your own money
- budget for and plan a school trip
- think about household spending and money saving tips.

Activity 1: Spending your money

Your father spends R5,00 on lotto tickets every Friday. Last Friday was his lucky day! He won R10 000 and gave you and your brother each R300 to spend.
You have never had so much money to spend and you want to plan the spending of your money carefully.

Think about those things that you really need to spend money on and those things which you would like to spend your money on, then
- draw up a table like the one below putting the most important things at the top of your list
- find out how much each item would cost by going to the shops or looking at advertisements in newspapers or magazines
- find the total cost of your needs and the total cost of your wants, then add these two totals together.

NEED	COST	WANT	COST
Bus Fare		Movie Ticket	
Shoes		Sweets	
....		....	
TOTAL		TOTAL	

You might have to change your plan. If your needs come to exactly R300 then you will not be able to spend any money on luxuries (your wants) unless you can get some of the things that you need at a lower cost. If your needs come to more than R300 you will not be able to have all the things that you need. Look again at your needs and discuss with a friend ways of spending less on these needs. Is there a cheaper way of getting to town? Are there shops which sell what you need at a lower price? Could you buy a different pair of shoes? Make a list of ways of economising (spending less money).

Discount

When doing the activity above, did you think about economising by buying on a sale when a discount is given?

Suppose that you have planned to spend R80 on a pair of shoes which you saw at Comfy Shoe Store.

When you arrive at the shop you are excited to see that there is a discount of 15% for cash.

You remember a conversation with your granny on a visit to town after Christmas last year.
Granny: Now is a good time to buy. There are lots of sales!
You: Why are there so many sales after Christmas?
Granny: People have spent a lot of money at Christmas and the shopkeepers are trying to get them to spend again.
You: This shop is giving 20% off the price of these jeans. How much is that?
Granny: Well 20% means 20 out of every 100 which is 1 out of every 5. So you will get one fifth off.
You: That means that instead of paying R75 for these jeans I will get one fifth off. That is R15 off.

What will you save on your shoes if you buy them at Comfy Shoes today?

How are you planning to spend the money that you saved?

Exercise 1

1. A lounge suite marked at R3 999,00 is sold for R3 500,00. What percentage discount is given? (Correct to one decimal place.)
2. Dr Mkhize's normal fee is R60 a visit but he gives patients who pay cash a discount of 10%. If you pay cash, what will you pay?
3. Cool Cats is selling Tommy Girl perfume at R249,99 for a 50 ml bottle. Saucy Sue sells the same perfume for R294,99 less 15% for cash. Which is the better cash price?
4. Swift and Safe motor car dealer offers a cash discount of 12% on second hand cars. What will a car marked at R5 999,99 cost you if you pay cash?

5. Electrical goods are advertised at a discount of 15% on a sale while furniture is sold at a 20% discount. Work out the price which you would pay for a fridge marked at R2 999,99 and a lounge suite marked at R3 499,99

Activity 2: Budgeting for your needs

(Work with your partner)

1. What is meant by 'budget'? Use a dictionary if you don't know.
2. Make a list of food which you might eat in one month and then work out the total cost of that food.
3. Discuss how much money has to be spent on your needs each month.
   Some things to consider are food, clothing, school fees and transport, but you may think of other things.
4. Draw up a table of all your needs and the likely cost of each.

NEED	COST
School fees	R10
Transport	R65
Food	. . . .
TOTAL	. . . .

5. Every year the cost of living increases. This means that everything costs more. If the expected increase in the cost of living for next year is 5%, add another column to your table showing the likely cost of your needs next year.

Exercise 2

1. If the rate of inflation is 5% per annum (every year), it means that on average the price of goods will increase by 5%. Find the likely cost for next year of:
   (a) a bicycle costing R399,99 now
   (b) a cooldrink costing R2,40 now
   (c) Nike shoes costing R499,99 now
   (d) jeans costing R129,99 now
2. 2,5 kg of sugar sold for R7,99 last year and is now selling at R8,88. What is the percentage increase in the price of sugar? (Give your answer correct to the nearest unit)

Activity 3: Starting a business from home

1. In a group discuss :
   (a) Ways in which you could make money from home. Some things you could consider are growing and selling vegetables, collecting and selling glass or newspaper, making and selling ice suckers, etc. Some of the things you need to think about before deciding on your business are:
   - do you have the right skills?
   - are there enough customers?

   (b) What costs would you have? Think about things like transport, goods you might have to buy to start your small business or equipment which you might need. These are called expenses. Where will you get this money?

   (c) How much money do you think that you could make each month? This is called income.

2. On your own now, draw up a simple budget for a business of your choice. One column should show expected income and another the expenses.

INVESTIGATE ■□■□■□■□

With a partner, plan a budget for a 3 day trip to a choir festival.

How will the costs of this trip be covered?
- Will there be fund-raising?
- Will sponsors be found?
- How much will choir members be expected to pay?
- Are there other ways of raising money for the trip?

Now add up all the amounts of money which you think you can raise. This sum is the income for your budget.

What are the expenses?
- Decide on a venue (how far will you have to travel?)
- Decide on the size of the choir
- Think about the transport (bus, mini bus taxi, train or car), the accommodation (where you will sleep), food and other expenses which may be necessary.
- Do some research about the costs that would be involved.
- Draw up a table similar to the one below. When you find the total of the expenses, make sure that your budget balances. This means that the total expenses must equal the total income.

INCOME		EXPENSES	
Fund raising		Transport	
Sponsors		Accommodation	
		Food	
TOTAL		TOTAL	

Activity 4: Household spending

(Work in a group or with a partner)

On your own read through the paragraph below and look carefully at the graph. If there are things which you do not understand, discuss them with members of the group. Then use the information given in the paragraph or in the graph to decide as a group whether you think that the statements at the top of the next page are true or not. Explain your answers.

South Africa has one of the most unequal sharings of income in the world. According to a PACSA factsheet of January 1998, a government survey published in October 1995 showed that 53% of the population have an income of less than R301 a month. This poor part of the population spends less than 10% of the money spent in the country, while the richest 5,8% of the population spends 40% of the money. The Sunday Times of 14 March 1999 reported on annual percentage increases in spending by the different population groups between 1993 and 1999 (see the graph). Although the spending by Black and Asian households is increasing at a much greater rate than in households of other population groups, the average Black household still spends only about 14% of what is spent by the average White household. Blacks who make up 78% of the population account for 43,8% of the spending while Whites who make up 10,6% of the population account for 43,1% of the spending.

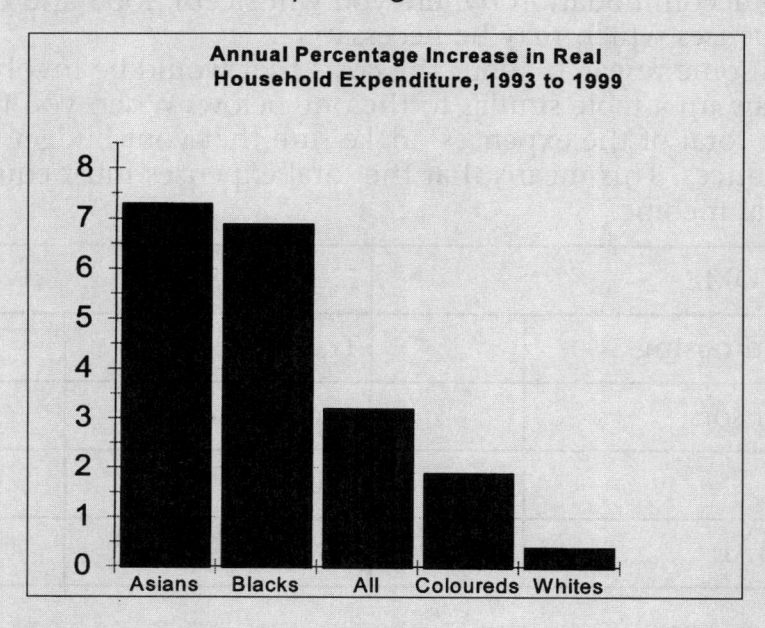

Annual Percentage Increase in Real Household Expenditure, 1993 to 1999

Group	Approx. %
Asians	7.3
Blacks	6.9
All	3.2
Coloureds	1.9
Whites	0.4

Are these statements true or false?

1. 47% of the population has an income of more than R301 a month.
2. The total amount of money spent by Whites and by Blacks is nearly the same.
3. The average White household spends about 7 times as much as the average Black household.
4. The annual percentage increase in spending in Black households is more than three times as much as in Coloured households.
5. The annual percentage increase in spending in Asian households is roughly the same as that of Blacks.

Activity 5: Household spending

(Work in a group or with a partner)

1. Look carefully at the pie graph below which shows overall household spending of South Africans in 1999.

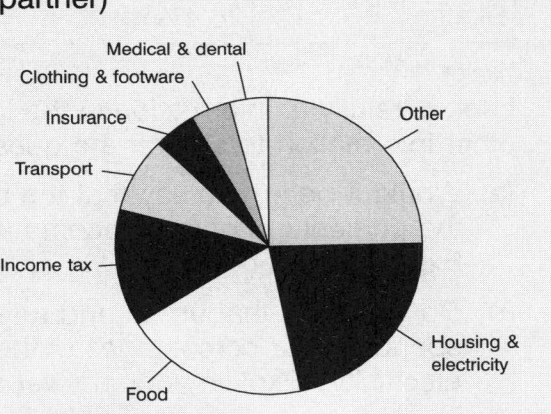

HOUSEHOLD SPENDING	
Medical and Dental	4,1%
Clothing and shoes	4,1%
Insurance Funds	4,1%
Transport	8,7%
Income Tax	12,5%
Food	19,7%
Housing and electricity	22,1%
Other	24,7%

(a) Discuss how you think that the percentages in the table on the previous page are likely to change in the case of very poor households. And in very rich households?

(b) Draw up tables which you think might show the percentage spending in poor and rich households.

2. The pie chart on the previous page shows that South Africans as a whole spend an average of 19,7% of their income on food and 22,1% on housing and electricity. The table below compares White and Black spending on these items.

	Food	Housing and electricity
Whites	12,4%	25,4%
Blacks	26,4%	18,4%

Look carefully at information in the table above and use it or any other information to answer the questions that follow.

(a) Would it be true to say that the poorer you are, the greater the percentage of your income that is spent on food? Explain your answer.

(b) Do you think that urban and rural Black households would spend similar percentages of their income on housing and electricity? Explain your answer.

(c) Why do you think that White households spend proportionately less on food and more on housing than Black households?

(d) Do you agree that food and housing are two of the most basic needs of all people?

(e) Make a list of the things on which money is spent in your home. Arrange your list in order (as you see it), from the most important to the least important need.

Activity 6: A family budget

Mr and Mrs Ntuli and their two teenagers Nkosinathi and Vusi live together. Here is their monthly budget. The income shown in the table is the money which they have left to take home once they have paid tax, U.I.F.(Unemployment Insurance Fund), medical aid and pension. This is known as Take-home Income.

INCOME	EXPENSES		
R1 500	CATEGORY	COST	PERCENT
	Food	R280,00	18,7%
	Transport	R270,00	
	School fees	R60,00	4%
	Funeral Insurance Policy	R50,00	
	Electricity	R90,00	6,0%
	Stokvel 1 (Food)	R50,00	
	Stokvel 2 (Savings)	R180,00	
	Retirement fund	R100,00	
	Other	R420,00	
	TOTAL	R1 500,00	100,0%

1. Discuss with your group:
   - How does a funeral insurance policy work?
   - What is a retirement fund?
   - How does a stokvel operate?
   - What kind of things might be included in the category 'other' in the budget?
2. Work out what percentage of their income the Ntuli's spend on each category and then discuss:
   - Do the Ntuli family spend a greater or smaller percentage of their income than the average South African family on food?
   - Do you think that there are categories for which too much or too little money is budgeted? If so, help them to adjust their budget.
   - Possible reasons why the Ntuli's appear to spend no money on housing.
3. A good budget plans for short term, medium term and long term needs. By long term we mean more than 5 years from now and by medium term between 1 and 5 years from now. Decide which items in the Ntuli budget are short term, medium term and long term.

Activity 7: Long term budgeting

Discuss in a group which items a family should consider when planning a long term budget.

Then think about your own particular family's needs. Decide:
- What items must be provided for?
- When will these items be needed?
- What is the likely cost of them at that stage?
- How can the budget make provision for them?

PROBLEM SOLVER

(Work in a group or with a partner)

The Ntuli's need to draw up a new budget. Mrs Ntuli is unwell and has taken unpaid sick leave from her work for 6 months. This means that her take-home income of R500 a month will now fall away. They do not wish to stop payment on the funeral policy or the retirement fund.

R125 a month will be saved on transport costs since Mrs Ntuli will not be travelling to work. Mrs Ntuli's mother is coming to live with them for 6 months and can afford to contribute R200 a month towards household expenses.

1. Work out what income the household now has, and then discuss in your group :

   - Which items in the Ntuli's budget will now cost more.

   - Cost effective ways of using electricity in the home.

   - How to get more from your money when shopping.

2. Draw up a new monthly budget putting it in a new table like the one in Activity 6.

3. Using different colours for the new and old budgets, draw one bar graph showing what percentage of their income the Ntuli's plan to spend on each category in the new and old budgets. Put the percentages on the vertical (up) axis and the categories on the horizontal (across) axis.

4. Are the old and new tables or the graph which you have drawn a more effective way of comparing the two budgets? Why do you think this?

How did you do?

- What section did you find most interesting? Why?
- Do you have some useful ideas on possible ways of earning money and how not to waste?
- Can you work out discount and percentage increase fairly easily?
- Do you have a good idea of how to plan and budget for a school trip?
- Were you able to interpret the written information and the graphs on household spending?
- Were you able to draw the bar graph easily so that you could compare the Ntuli's old and new budgets?
- Do you understand what is meant by, and the effect of, inflation on a budget?
- Do you understand what is meant by long term budgeting?
- Do you understand what is meant by luxuries and necessities?

UNIT 4

Furnishing a Flat

If you look around your home, you will see many objects, appliances and furnishings that have different shapes, for example, beds, plates, the T.V., a table. Can you think of any others? Name 5 examples. What shapes can you identify in the picture above? If you want to buy a bed or a cupboard, it is useful to know the measurements or be able to estimate the space it will take up. If you want to carpet a room or tile a floor, you need to find the surface area of that room so that you can calculate the cost. Area is the space taken up by a flat or curved surface. It is measured in units such as square centimetres (cm^2) or square metres (m^2) The boundary around an area is called the perimeter. The perimeter is measured in units such as centimetres (cm) or metres(m).

In this unit you will be given the opportunity to:

- understand and calculate the area and perimeter of circles, rectangles, parallelograms and triangles
- learn to estimate (to give a rough calculation which is more or less correct)
- learn to find the cost of tiling an area or carpeting a floor
- create and design a bedroom using scale drawings.

Activity 1: Tiling

The following tiles cover an area behind the sink in the kitchen.

Each little tile is 5cm by 5cm. The area of each tile is 25cm². (5cm x 5cm) What is the area of the rectangle? What rule can you use to find the area of a rectangle?

Example: Find the area of the rectangular floor tile.

Solution: Area = length x breadth
= 9 x 5
= 45 cm²

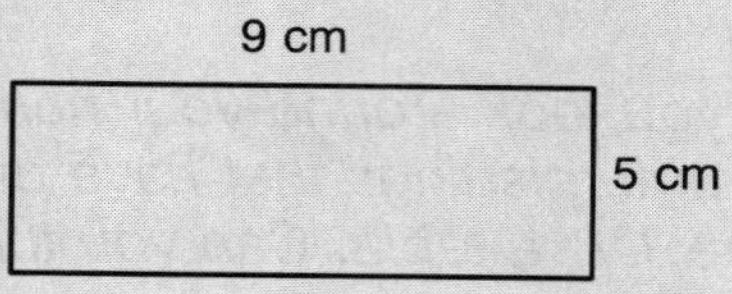

9 cm

5 cm

Exercise 1

Find the area of each of the following tiles (measurements in cm).

1.

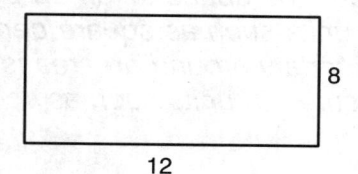

8

12

2.

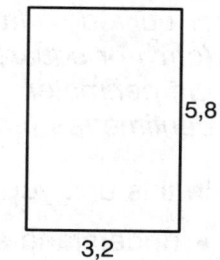

5,8

3,2

3.

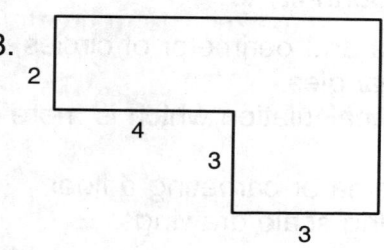

2

4

3

3

Activity 2: How large is my flat?

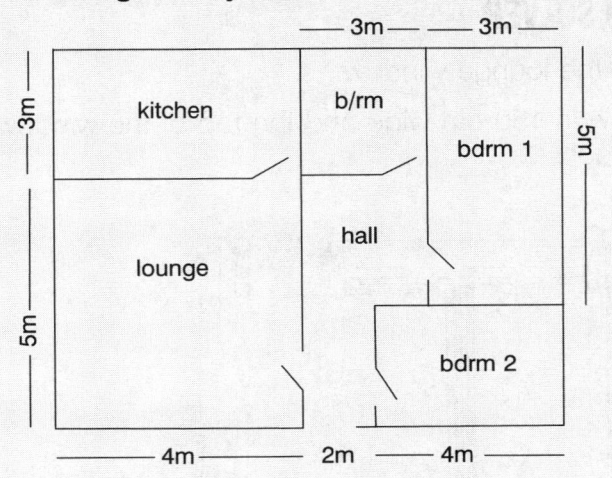

Above is a floor plan of a 2 bedroom flat. Work in pairs to discuss and answer the following questions.

Do you think it is a good design? How do you think it could be improved?

Calculate the following;

1. the area of the kitchen
2. the area of the hall
3. the total area of the flat
4. the perimeter of the hall
5. the perimeter of the flat
6. the cost of carpeting the lounge floor at R56,50 per m^2
7. the cost of tiling the kitchen and bathroom floors at R42,00 per m^2
8. the cost of building the flat if the builder quotes a price of R1200,00 per m^2

You decide to leave 1 metre of flooring around the perimeter of bedroom 2.

9. What area of the floor will be covered by a carpet?
10. What area is left uncovered?

PROBLEM SOLVER

Curtaining the lounge window.

The window is 150 cm wide and the top of the window is 235 cm from the floor.

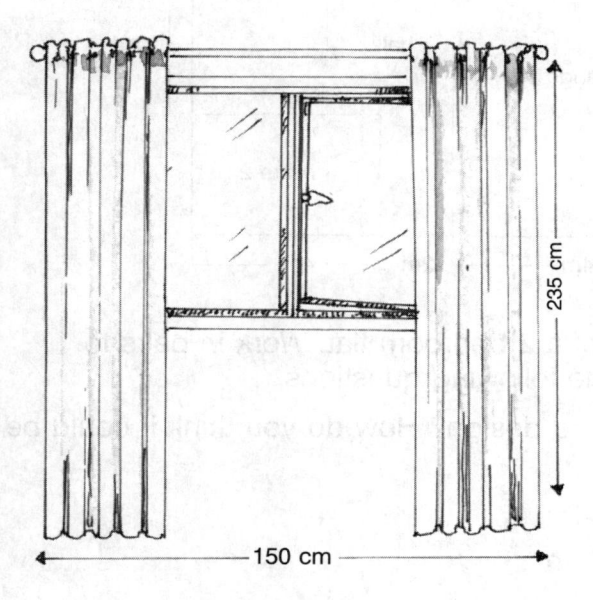

The curtain (drop) on each side of the window must be twice the width of the window to give the curtains fullness.

1. How wide must each drop be?
2. If you need 40 cm extra for the hem and tape, what will the actual length of the drop be?
   Curtain material can be 115 cm or 150 cm wide.
3. Calculate the amount of material (in metres) needed if you use (a) 115 cm wide material and (b) 150 cm wide material. Use a sketch to help you reach your answers.
   The materials you like cost R36,00 per metre (115 cm wide) and R42,00 per metre (150 cm wide).
4. Which would be the more economical (cheaper) option?

Activity 3: Find the area of a parallelogram

You will need an empty cereal box, scissors, tape.

Work in pairs.

Cut out the back and front of the cereal box carefully and keep the two rectangular shapes to one side. You should have a rectangular frame. Slant the frame to one side. What shape have you formed? What do you notice about the height? How does it change? As the height gets smaller, what happens to the area? Does the change in height affect the perimeter?

Take one of the rectangular pieces of the cereal box and cut a triangle off it. Rearrange the two pieces to form a parallelogram. What do you notice about the heights of the rectangle and the parallelogram? What do you notice about their areas? We say that the area of a parallelogram is base x perpendicular height.

Example. ABCD is a parallelogram. Find the area.

Solution. Area = base x height
= 6 x 4
= 24 cm²

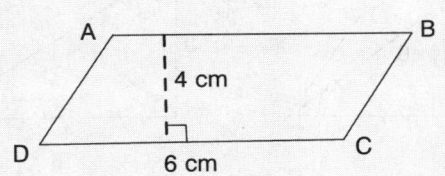

Exercise 2

Find the area of the following parallelograms. (measurements in cm)

1. S, T, U, V; 8, 12

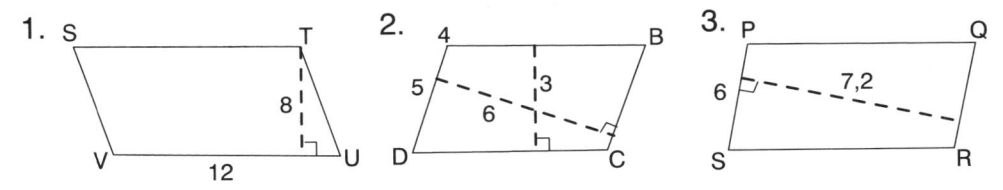

2. 4, 5, 3, 6; B, C, D

3. P, Q, R, S; 6, 7,2

Find

(a) the area of PQRS

(b) the height when PS is the base.

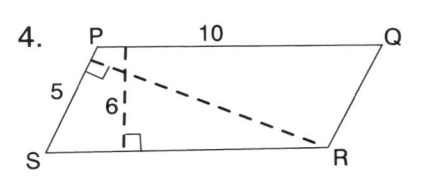

4. P, Q, R, S; 10, 5, 6

Activity 4: Find the area of a triangle

Take the back of the cereal box and cut it in half from corner to corner. What shapes have you formed? What do you think the word triangle means? Can you think of any other words beginning with tri? What can you say about the area of a triangle and the area of a rectangle? What can you work out about the area of a triangle and the area of a parallelogram?

We say that the area of a triangle = $\frac{1}{2}$ base x perpendicular height.

Example: Find the area of ABC.

Solution Area = $\frac{1}{2}$ base x height
= $\frac{1}{2}$ x 6 x 4
= 12 cm^2

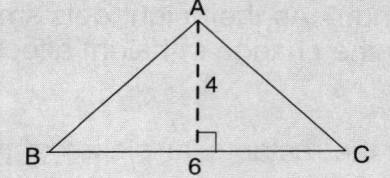

Exercise 3

Find the area of the following triangles.(measurements in cm)

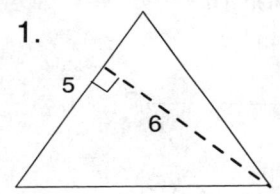

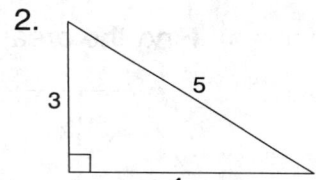

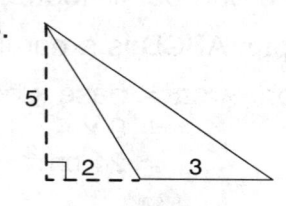

1.
2.
3.

Activity 5: Design a wall hanging

Design a wall hanging for the lounge wall using rectangles, triangles and parallelograms in your design. Make use of colour and be imaginative.
The Ndebele painting in Unit 1 may inspire you.
The design below is painted above the front door of the flat.
How many triangles are there in the design?

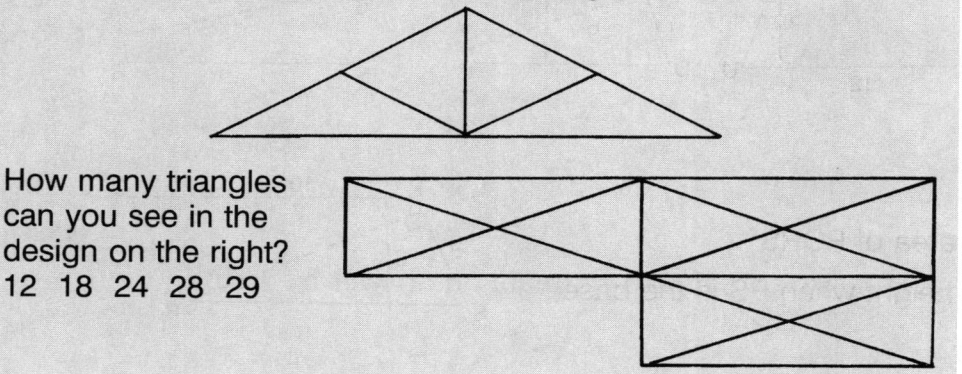

How many triangles can you see in the design on the right?
12 18 24 28 29

A design project: your ideal bedroom

You have entered a competition that requires you to design your ideal bedroom. Prepare a rough sketch of your ideal bedroom.

Complete a scale drawing of the floor area.

Refer to magazines, newspapers, etc. to choose new furniture.

Use pieces of cardboard to represent furniture.

List all the items in your room.

Calculate the cost of all the items required to furnish your room including items like bed linen, lamps, mirrors, etc.

Work on A4 paper and present your design project as a booklet. It should be about 3 or 4 pages long.

Good luck for the competition!

INVESTIGATE ■□■□■□■□■□

What is pi?

1. Measure (using string and then measuring the length of the string) the circumference of 3 circular objects, for example, a cup, a coin, a bicycle wheel.
2. Measure the diameter of each object.
3. Calculate the ratio of circumference ÷ diameter of each.
4. What do you notice? Is the ratio more or less the same each time?
5. Roughly how many diameters equal the circumference?

   Did you find that the circumference (length) of a circle is a little more than 3 times as long as its diameter? It is about 3,14 times as long and this number is called 'pi' or π. More precisely 'pi' is

   3,14159265358979323846264338327950

   But even this is not exact. Does pi ever repeat itself in a pattern? Does it ever end? What kind of number is pi?

6. If π = circumference ÷ diameter, what is the rule to find the circumference of a circle, given the diameter or radius?

We can write it as : $C = \pi \times d$ or $C = 2\pi \times r$

It is often useful to estimate an answer by rounding off numbers and doing a quick calculation in your head. What would you round off π to?

Example: Estimate the circumference of the plate and then calculate the answer.

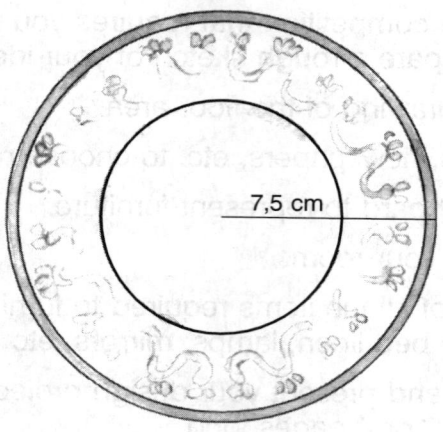

7,5 cm

Estimated answer
Circumference = 3 × 15
            = 45 cm

Actual answer
Circumference = π × d
            = π × 15
            = 47,12 cm

Exercise 4

1. Estimate, then calculate the circumference of a circular mat with radius 1,5 m.

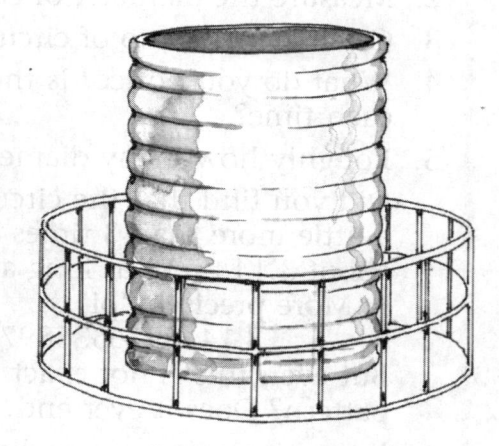

2. Outside the flat is a water tank with a diameter of 3 m. What is the circumference of the water tank?

3. Your father wants to build a fence around the water tank. The fence must be 1 m from the water tank. How much fencing must he buy?

4. A circular table with height 70 cm and diameter 50 cm needs a circular tablecloth that will drape to the floor. What is the diameter of the tablecloth?
5. How much lace is needed to go round the edge of the circular tablecloth?
6. Imagine that you had a circular tablecloth that fitted exactly the top of the table. What would the shape of the extra piece that fits around the table look like? What would its measurements be?

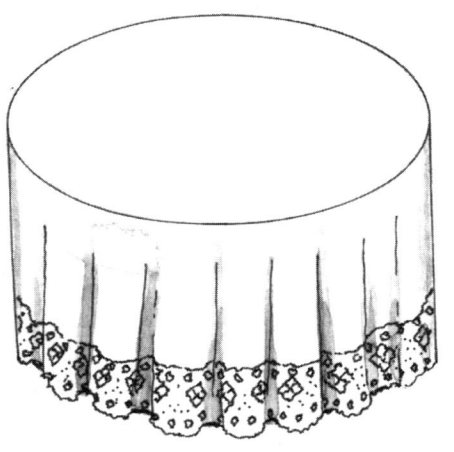

PROBLEM SOLVER

Behind your flat is an old tree that needs to be cut down. Your father has borrowed a chainsaw with a blade of length 45 cm. He uses a tape measure to measure the circumference of the tree and finds it is 250 cm. How far into the tree does the blade go? With care, it is possible to cut down a tree if the blade reaches the centre. Will he be able to cut down the tree?

Finding the age of a tree.

Every year as a tree grows, its trunk expands in concentric circles.

These growth rings vary according to the weather conditions during any particular year. However, the circumference of the trunk increases, on average, by 2,5 cm every year. How would you estimate the age of a tree without chopping it down or using π? How old, roughly, was the tree that your father has cut down?

You decide to plant a new tree to replace the old one. You buy a tree with a circumference of 25 cm. Estimate how old the tree is. About how many years will it take to develop the same circumference as the one that was cut down? Why do you think it is important to plant trees?

Area of a circle.

The area of a circle is given by the formula: Area = πr^2

Example: The area of a circular plate with radius of 15 cm is:

Area = $\pi \times (15)^2$
     = 706,86cm^2

Exercise 5

1. Find the area of the circular reed mats below.

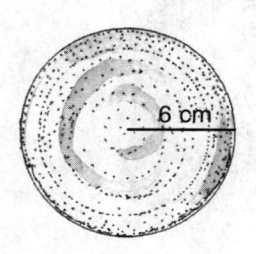

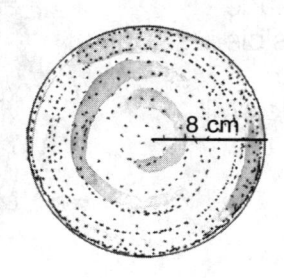

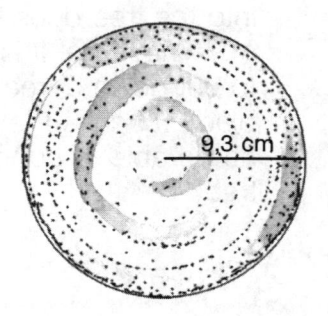

   6 cm   8 cm   9,3 cm

2. Bedroom 2 in the flat has a circular mat on the floor with diameter 1,8m. What area of floor is uncovered?

PROBLEM SOLVER

I need a round table to go in the lounge. It must be able to seat 8 people. Each person takes up 0,5 m around the edge of the table. How large must the circumference be? What area will it take up in the lounge? Would it fit easily into the kitchen?

Mirror, mirror on the wall

Can you complete the next line? Who is speaking?

Unfortunately, the glass in your mirror in the bathroom has broken.

Calculate the area of glass needed to replace it.

The wooden frame is 2 cm wide.

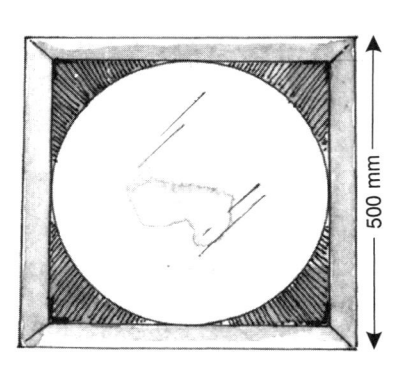

How did you do?

- Do you feel that you can calculate areas and perimeters/circumferences fairly easily?
- Were you satisfied with your design project? Did you struggle with any part of it? How did it compare with those of your peers?
- Which section did you find the most interesting?

UNIT 5

Who is top of the log?

There are many situations in life where we need to be able to compare two things together. We also often need to be able to show our comparison to other people, so we need to be able to put this information into some sort of a chart so that others can easily see the results of our survey. Find out the results of 4 soccer teams that members of your class support. Find out how many games have been played this season and what the results are. Discuss what the best way to display your data will be.

In this unit you will:

- learn how to draw a pie chart
- learn how to draw a bar graph
- learn how to draw a line graph
- learn how to draw a frequency bar graph
- learn how to draw a frequency polygon
- use the above graphs to read off data
- decide which is the best graph to use in a situation.

The pie chart

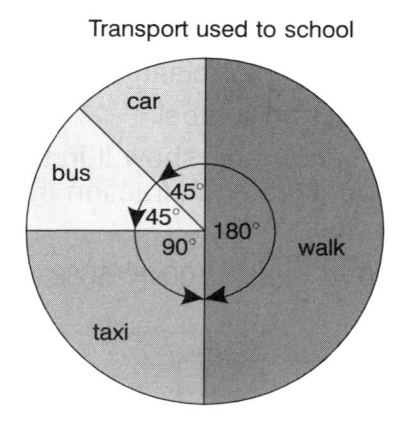

Transport used to school

Above is a pie chart that shows which transport learners in a school use. The complete circle shows the total number of learners.

The table shows the information collected:

walk	taxi	car	bus
Total	300	150	75
75	600		

To draw this pie chart:
1. To work out each sector of the pie, take

$$\frac{\text{number who walk}}{\text{total}} \times 360° = \frac{300}{600} \times 360° = 180°$$

$$\frac{\text{number who use a taxi}}{\text{total}} \times 360° = \frac{150}{600} \times 360° = 90°$$

$$\frac{\text{number who use a car}}{\text{total}} \times 360° = \frac{75}{600} \times 360° = 45°$$

$$\frac{\text{number who use a bus}}{\text{total}} \times 360° = \frac{75}{600} \times 360° = 45°$$

Check that all the degrees add up to 360°, which is the total degrees in a circle.

2. Now, draw a circle using a compass. (Make it at least $\frac{1}{3}$ page)
3. Draw a line through the centre of the circle.
4. Measure each sector using a protractor, 180° for walking, 90° for the taxi, 45° for bus and 45° for car.
5. Add colour or patterns to show each sector clearly.
6. Label each sector and give the pie chart a label.
7. Work out the percentage of each sector and show it in the sector. To work out the percentage, take each fraction from number 1 and x 100 instead of x 360°.

i.e. $\frac{\text{number who walk}}{\text{total}} \times 100 = \frac{300}{600} \times 100 = 50\%$

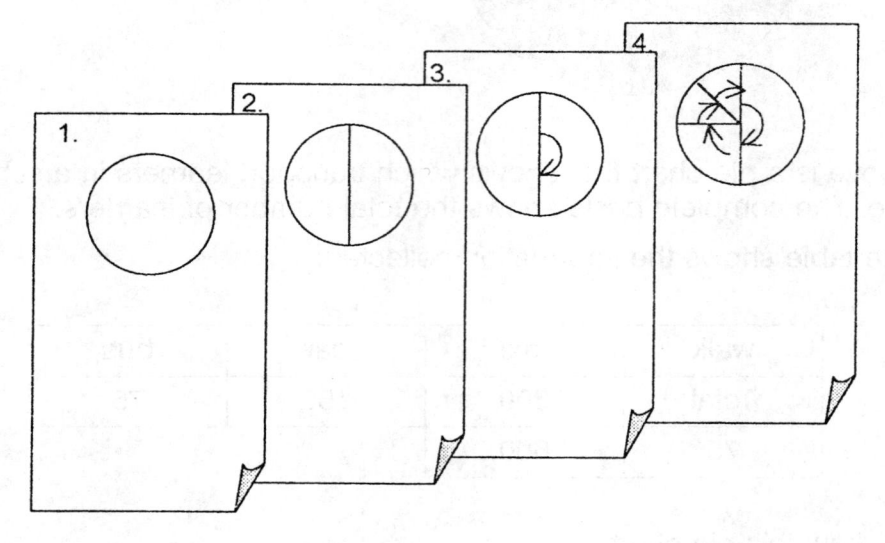

Exercise 1

You are given the following table that shows the results of 4 soccer teams in a league

	Won	Drawn	Lost	Played
Morocco Swallows	3	2	1	6
Amazulu	2	2	2	6
Orlando Pirates	1	1	2	4
Kaizer Chiefs	1	1	2	4

(a) Draw 3 pie charts to show what percentage of their games Amazulu, Pirates and Chiefs have won, drawn or lost. The pie chart for Swallows has been done as an example:

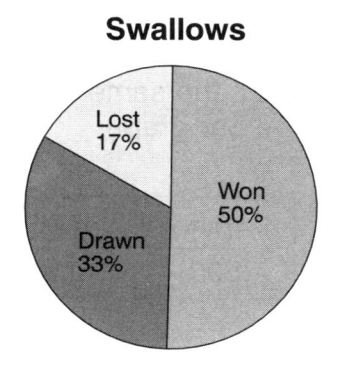

Swallows

- Won 50%
- Drawn 33%
- Lost 17%

(b) Draw another 3 pie charts to show the percentage of games that each team has drawn, lost and played. The pie chart for the percentage of games won by each team has been done as an example:

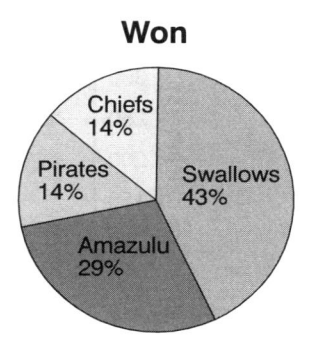

Won

- Swallows 43%
- Amazulu 29%
- Pirates 14%
- Chiefs 14%

Activity 1: Draw your own pie chart

- Work in pairs.
- Decide on a topic that you think is useful to collect and represent data about. You could collect data about a school sports team and their position in the log; you could decide to investigate types of food learners eat at lunch time; or types of cars teachers drive. Try to think of something original that all your classmates will not be researching as well.
- Collect the data and then display it in a pie chart. There may be more than one pie chart that you can do. Decide what you want your results to show and do a pie chart that supports your opinion.

The bar graph

We will use the same table showing transport to school to learn about the bar graph.

walk	taxi	car	bus	Total
300	150	75	75	600

The bar graph showing how learners get to school is shown below:

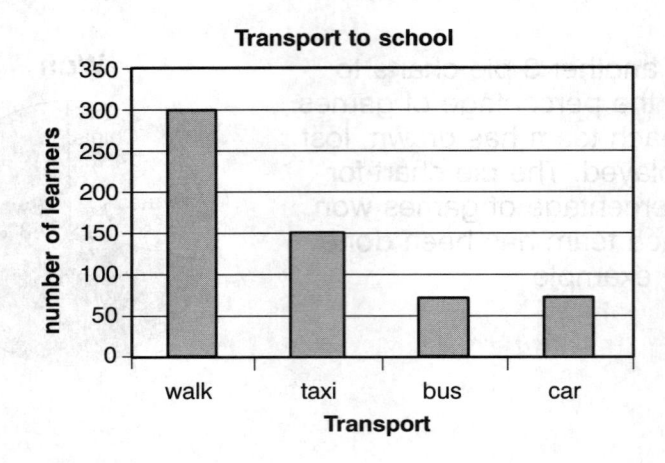

Transport to school

To draw the bar graph:

1. Use about $\frac{1}{3}$ of a page, or use graph paper.
2. Label the x axis (horizontal or across axis) with the type of transport. Make sure that the width of the columns is the same.
3. Label the y axis (vertical or up axis) with the numbers. Look at the highest and lowest numbers on the table before you start. You should always try to start the y axis values at 0, and then go up in equal spaces until you get to the highest value.
4. Put a label on the x axis, the y axis and at the top of the graph.
5. Draw the bars in with a pencil, and make sure they are drawn accurately before you colour them in with patterns or colours.

Exercise 2

Use the following table showing soccer results

	Won	Drawn	Lost	Played
Swallows	3	2	1	6
Amazulu	2	2	2	6
Pirates	1	1	2	4
Chiefs	1	1	2	4

Draw bar graphs that show
(a) how many games each team won
(b) how many games each team drew
(c) how many games each team lost
(d) the results of Swallows
(e) the results of Amazulu
(f) the results of Pirates
(g) the results of Chiefs.

Activity 2: Draw your own bar graph

- Work in pairs.
- Decide on a topic that you think is useful to collect and represent data about. You could collect data about a school sports team and their position in the log; you could decide to investigate types of food learners eat at lunch time; or types of cars teachers drive. Try to think of something original that all your class mates will not be researching as well.
- Collect the data and then display it in a bar graph. There may be more than one bar graph that you can do. Decide what you want your results to show and do a bar graph that supports your opinion.

The line graph

We will use a table showing temperature changes over 4 days in hospital to learn about the line graph.

Monday	Tuesday	Wednesday	Thursday
41°	38°	$36\frac{1}{2}°$	$36\frac{1}{2}°$

The line graph showing temperature changes is shown below:

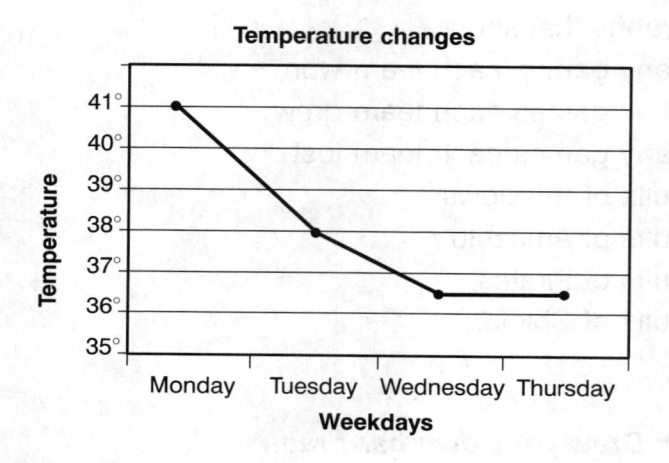

Temperature changes

(Graph showing temperature on y-axis from 35° to 41° and Weekdays on x-axis: Monday 41°, Tuesday 38°, Wednesday 36½°, Thursday 36½°)

To draw the line graph:
1. Use about $\frac{1}{3}$ of a page, or use graph paper.
2. Label the x axis with the days of the week. Use a fixed number of centimetres for the x axis so that your graph is uniform (looks even).
3. Label the y axis with the temperatures. Look at the highest and lowest temperatures on the table before you start. You cannot start the y axis values at 0 so start at 35° and then go up in equal spaces until you get to the highest value.
4. Put a label on the x axis, the y axis and at the top of the graph.
5. Mark a cross where each value must go in the middle of that column. Join the crosses up using a ruler and a sharp pencil. The line that is formed is sometimes called a 'broken line' graph, or a 'jagged line' graph.

Exercise 3

1. The following table shows the rainfall in Durban for the year 1998. Draw a line graph to show this data.

	Jan	Feb	Mar	Apr	May	Jun	Jul	Aug	Sept	Oct	Nov	Dec
Rainfall mm	90	100	85	50	55	50	45	50	180	150	120	100

2. The following table shows the temperature for a city in KwaZulu-Natal over a summer month. Draw a line graph to represent this data.

Date	1	2	3	4	5	6	7	8	9	10	11	12	13	14	15	16	17	18	19	20	21	22	23	24	25	26	27	28
Temp °C	31	26	27	26	32	30	28	29	35	34	31	27	24	22	23	24	25	22	23	26	27	28	31	34	33	31	30	29

The frequency bar graph (frequency histogram)

Below is a table showing the results of a class in a test. The number of learners in each category (range of marks) has been tallied up and shown in the table. This is called the frequency – how many times a certain mark comes up.

Next to the table the frequency bar graph has been drawn.

Mark	Number of learners
0-20	1
21-40	7
41-60	22
61-80	14
81-100	7

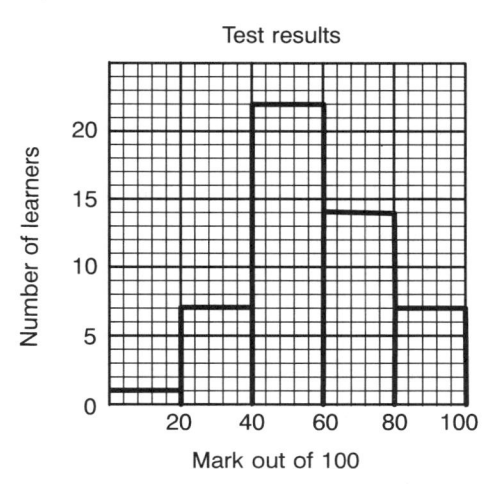

The frequency bar graph is drawn in the same way as the normal bar graph, with one difference. In the frequency bar graph, the data is related (continuous) so the bars are drawn next to each other, without the gap between them that you see in the normal bar graph.

The frequency polygon

A polygon is a many sided enclosed figure.

A frequency polygon is the same as a frequency bar graph, but now instead of columns we use points. All the points are joined together as in the line graph, but are also joined to the x axis at the beginning and at the end.
In the example, the first data point is for data between 0 and 20, so the point is put in the middle of the column. The line is extended back to the x axis in the middle of the previous column, which in this case is at 0. At the end, the line is extended forwards to the centre of the next column, so it joins the x axis at 100.

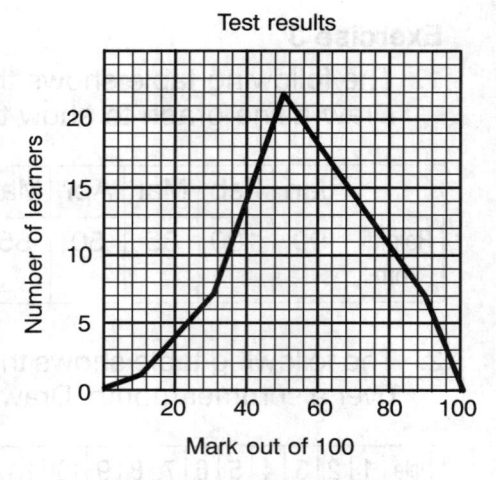

Activity 3: Graph your own test results

1. Draw a bar graph showing the results for your class in the last test. Get the data from your class teacher.
2. Draw a frequency polygon using the same data.
3. Draw a frequency bar graph showing the results of the whole of grade 8 in the last maths test. Are the results very different from your class results? If they are, why do you think this is so?

INVESTIGATE ■□■□■□■□■□

- Choose a sport that your school plays. It may be soccer, netball, cricket or rugby.
- In pairs, draw up a table which shows how many games you have played this season, and show how many games you have won, drawn and lost.
- Show these results in any chart.
- Now work out a tally table to find out the opinion of learners in your school about whether your school will be top of the log in that sport. You need to design a tally table, decide on the size sample that will be big enough to find out the school opinion, and then show the results using a different type of chart to the one used before.

How to decide what type of graph to draw

1. Pie charts are used best when you want to show data that must be represented as a percentage of a total. Can you add all the data up to get a meaningful total? If the answer is yes, then use a pie chart.

Examples:
- to show what percentage of the class has 2 siblings, 3 siblings, 4 siblings
- to show what percentage of matches was won, lost and drawn
- to show what percentage of land is used for agriculture, housing and other
- to show what percentage of people at a function are boys, girls and adults.

2. Use a bar graph to show comparisons of things that you can't add up to get a total.

Examples:
- to show a comparison of heights of mountains
- to show a comparison of marks for different subjects
- to show a comparison rainfall in different months.

3. Line graphs are used when there is some kind of connection between the pieces of data.

Examples:
- temperatures of a patient in hospital
- rainfall in different months
- profit of a company over a number of consecutive years.

4. Frequency bar graphs and polygons are used when there is a connection between the data and the y axis shows how often something happens. The y axis is usually labelled 'number of . . .' or 'frequency'.

Examples:
- test or exam results for a particular subject or class
- any data collected which needs a comparison of how often something occurs.

Exercise 4

1. At the beginning of unit 2 you completed a tally table in the section **How democracy works** on votes counted for each political party at the last election. Draw a pie chart showing the spread of votes.
2. In the INVESTIGATION for Unit 2 you collected data from your class, your grade and your school on types of transport used. Decide which type of chart to draw for each one and then draw the chart.
3. In Unit 2 you also used a stem and leaf plot to display data. Draw a frequency polygon to display the data that you used in the first stem and leaf plot. Use a double frequency bar graph to show the data for the back to back stem and leaf plot.

PROBLEM SOLVER

The Soweto Swingers are a new soccer team in town. They are playing in the Premier Soccer League and need an average home game attendance of 8000. This will make enough money to keep the team playing. Attendances at their first 6 home games were: 9100; 9800; 4900; 6700; 5300; 4400

a) Estimate, then calculate, the average attendance at the first 6 games. The Swingers have 7 home games left. They must get enough supporters at the games or the team will collapse.

b) What must the average attendance for the last 7 games be, for the team to survive?

How did you do?

- Did you manage to draw all the different types of graphs?
- Did you understand how to choose a type of graph?
- Could you work out the percentages in the pie charts?
- Which section did you find the most useful?
- Is there any part of this unit that you don't understand? Discuss this with a friend and see if you can understand it better now.
- Which part of this unit did you find the most interesting? Why?
- Which part of this unit was the most challenging? Why?

UNIT 6

What's cooking in the kitchen?

The recipes and menus that appear in cookery books are usually intended for four or six people. If we need to prepare a meal for one or two people, or for a large crowd, we have to be able to adjust the recipe. We have to scale the quantities listed in the recipe up or down. We also have to be able to measure the different ingredients which are required in the recipe. If we're lucky, we will find the right measuring equipment in the kitchen; measuring jugs, flasks or cups. If we're not fortunate enough to have all the right equipment, we may need to improvise, to use other items in the kitchen. Sometimes we might have to estimate, or guess the approximate measurement of an ingredient.

In this unit you will be given the opportunity to:

- use different measuring techniques to produce the correct quantities of ingredients
- convert temperatures from one scale to the other
- understand what is meant by ratio and proportion
- design and construct measuring and cooking equipment
- plan and draw up suitable menus.

Measuring Temperature

In cookery it is important to be able to set the oven to the correct temperature. Gas cookers are usually regulated using gas marks, and electric cookers are marked in degrees Fahrenheit (°F) or degrees Celsius (°C). The following table shows the most commonly used oven temperatures that appear in cookery books.

Gas mark:	°C	°F
3	170	325
4	180	350
5	190	375
6	200	400
7	220	425

What is the approximate relationship between degrees Celsius and degrees Fahrenheit? In other words, how much bigger or smaller is the one than the other?

What would the °C and °F readings be for gas mark 1?

The conversions from Celsius to Fahrenheit are only approximate. It is worth knowing how to convert accurately from one temperature to another. Here is the method for moving from Fahrenheit to Celsius.

1. First take 32 away from the F temperature.
2. Multiply your answer by 5.
3. Divide the answer by 9.

Think for a moment. Does it matter if you do step 2 before you do step 1?

We can actually write this conversion as

$$°C = \frac{5(°F - 32)}{9}$$

When you need to convert from °C to °F, you do the exact opposite to the steps on page 58. You first multiply by 9, then divide by 5, and finally add on 32. Try these.

Exercise 1

1. 10 °C   2. 30 °C   3. 42 °C   4. - 10 °C   5. -20 °C

INVESTIGATE ■□■□■□■□■□

What happens to water when it freezes? Does its volume increase or decrease? Do the following. Half fill a tall, regular shaped glass with water. Now add three ice cubes. Mark the level of the water with a piece of tape on the side of the glass. Allow the ice to melt. Once all the ice has melted, check the level of the water. Has it risen, fallen, or stayed the same?

Now find a regular shaped bottle (see the drawing alongside) and mark on a piece of tape the 2, 3, 4 cm levels up to 6 cm. Stick this to the side of the bottle, fill the bottle with water to the 4 cm mark, and put the bottle in the freezer. Once it has frozen, take it out and note the new level.
Calculate the fractional increase or decrease in volume as follows;

$$\frac{\text{2nd reading} - \text{1st reading}}{\text{1st reading}}$$

What about this?

Water freezes at 0 degrees Celsius and boils at 100 degrees Celsius. What do you think the temperature would be on a very hot summer's afternoon in Kimberley?

What should our normal body temperature read on the thermometer?

What do you think the temperature inside a normal kitchen refrigerator would be?

Water boils at 100°C at sea level. At the top of Mount Everest, it boils at 80°C. You usually like your egg to cook for 3 minutes. Assuming you manage to climb Mount Everest, and choose to stop for a while to have some breakfast, should you boil your egg for longer or shorter than 3 minutes?

The class lunch

Exercise 2

You and your friend have been given the responsibility of preparing a lunch for your class of 40. You have decided that the lunch will consist of savoury mince, potatoes, carrots and green beans, followed by rice pudding, coffee or tea.

Your cookery book gives the following recipes to feed four people:

Savoury mince 500g minced beef
250g onions
200g tinned tomatoes
cornflour, salt
pepper, paprika.

Rice pudding: 125g round grain rice
60g sugar
625mℓ milk

1. Assuming that you have sufficient salt, pepper, paprika and cornflour, work out the quantities of the other ingredients needed for the savoury mince and the rice pudding.
2. The cookery book also suggests the following:
   500g potatoes serves three people
   500g carrots serves four people
   500g beans serves four people.

How many kilograms of each of these vegetables do you need? Remember, 1 kilogram = 1000 grams.

3. A litre of milk will supply 20 cups of tea, 6 tea bags will make a pot of tea for 15 people, and a 100g jar of coffee provides 50 cups.

Calculate what you need if:
- everyone decides to have tea
- everyone has coffee
- the number of coffee drinkers is double that of the tea drinkers.

PROBLEM SOLVER

You need to measure out certain volumes of orange squash cooldrink for some friends. You have no measuring jugs with markings on them but you do have a 3 litre and a 5 litre jug.

Hlow would you use these jugs to arrive at the following volumes?

2 litres
6 litres
4 litres
1 litres

Ratio and proportion

A ratio shows how many times one quantity is bigger than the other. The ratio of two quantities can be calculated by dividing them. For example, if a cake contains 180g of flour and 60g of butter, it is said to contain flour and butter in the ratio of 3:1 (180 divided by 60).

A ratio is a comparison of different amounts of the same thing. In a soft drink, the ratio of cordial (cold drink) to water might be one part to four parts, written as 1:4. In cookery, the taste and the texture (find out what this word means) depends very much on the relationship or ratio between the ingredients, rather than how much is used.

Ratios can often be simplified by expressing them in smaller numbers. So, 4 grams of sugar compared with 12 grams of salt, is the same as 1 gram of sugar compared with 3 grams of salt, means sugar and salt in the ratio 1:3.

Using the symbol : simplify these ratios.

Exercise 3

1. 8 gram compared with 14 gram
2. 16 litres compared with 24 litres
3. 2,5 kilograms compared with 4 kilograms
4. 3,2 millilitres compared with 4 millilitres
5. R5 compared with R7,50

When the units are not the same, it is best to change the larger unit to the smaller one.

So, 4 kilograms : 800 grams becomes 4000 grams : 800 grams becomes 5 : 1.

Try the following conversions to see whether you understand how to convert and simplify.

6. 3 kilograms : 600 grams
7. 240 ml : 1,8 litres
8. 0,2 kg : 80 grams
9. 2 cups : 3 half cups
10. 3 Tbs : 6 tsp   1 Tbs (tablespoon) = 5 tps (teaspoons).

Sharing the pie - and the cake!

Your mother has baked two large round ham and cheese pies for you and your five friends. She has asked you to divide these two pies equally so that each of you not only receives the same amount of pie but also the same shape! Draw these two pies and show how you would divide them.

What if your mother baked a fruit cake for you and your two brothers, and said that you had to share it among the three of you in the ratio 1 : 2 : 3? How would you divide the cake? Explain to your classmate, or whoever sits nearest to you, how you got the answer.

The fruit cake baked by your mother contains flour, sugar, butter and dried fruit in the following proportions **by weight**. (Proportion is just another way of talking about ratios. Where the quantities are always in the same ratio, we say they are in proportion.)
The proportions are 4 : 2 : 2 : 3.
If the cake mixture weighs 1,76 kg, what is the weight of each ingredient? Why was it important to mention the words in bold?

Activity 1: Making a measure

How would you make a simple cardboard container that would allow you to measure accurately different amounts (volumes) of sugar, flour etc.? The volumes should range between 50 ml and 500 ml. Write down the various steps in this 'design and make" activity, as if it was a set of instructions for someone else.
For example, the instructions could start off as follows: "Take a piece of cardboard, about ... mm thick, ... mm long and ... mm wide. With your ruler, mark ..."

PROBLEM SOLVER

You are the owner of a bakery that makes delicious pies. Your sister takes the orders and collects the money for the pies. You bake the pies in the kitchen at the back of your shop. You spend 5 hours each day baking pies, and are able to produce 140 pies. Your pies are so popular, that you cannot meet the demands (needs) of your customers. You have to employ your friend Michael to help you bake pies. He is not as quick as you and can only produce 20 pies per hour. He also bakes for 5 hours each day.

1. How many pies are baked each day?
2. How many pies are baked each hour?
3. If you hire one more person, who bakes twice as quickly as Michael, how many pies will you be able to supply each day?
4. If the demand for pies increases to 3000 per week (5 days), what will you have to do? There is no more space in the kitchen.

How did you do?

- Could you do the Celsius to Fahrenheit conversions fairly easily?
- Did you get the egg problem right? If not, where did you go wrong?
- How did your "design and make" product compare with the others in the class?
- Which section did you find the most interesting? Why?
- Is there any part of this unit which still bothers you?

UNIT 7

Finding our way with Maps

Have you ever been lost in a big city, or in open country? Not knowing your way can be very frightening! To help us find our way, being able to use a compass and to read maps are very useful. They tell us where we can expect to find the places that we want to find, how far and in what direction we must go, and they also tell us many things about what we can expect to see on the way there.

- Have **you** ever been lost? Share your own experiences with members of your group.
- In our modern world there are many things to help people avoid getting lost, and to help them if they do become lost. Can you think of some of them? Make a list of them.

In this unit you will have the opportunity to:

- estimate and measure lengths and distances
- use direction N, S, E, W as well as NE, NW, etc.
- draw simple maps
- use grid references to find places on a map
- use scale to find the actual distance between places on a map.

Activity 1: Drawing a map

1. Your uncle from another province is coming to visit your family and you have been asked to draw a rough map of your area to help him find places which he may need to visit.

   (a) Estimate (guess) the approximate distance and direction of the following places from your home: your school; the nearest clinic, doctor or hospital; the nearest police station; the nearest public telephone; the nearest shop; at least one other feature (place) of your choice.

   (b) Draw a simple map showing all these features.

2. In your group
   - look at one another's maps
   - do you think you could find your way using these maps?
   - is there anything that you particularly like about any of the maps?

3. Self Assessment
   - Have you shown the position of all the places which you needed to include on your map?
   - Have you marked any special features such as rivers, special buildings, etc which your uncle would pass on his way to places?
   - Does your map tell your uncle in what direction to go in order to get to places?
   - Can he use your map to find out approximately how far he must go to get to places?
   - What problems might your uncle have when using your map?
   - Do you need any new knowledge or skills which would help you to improve your map?

4. In your group report back and discuss difficulties you have in trying to improve your map.

Measuring lengths

Activity 2: Measuring lengths

1. What units would you use to measure:
   (a) the length and breadth of the pages of this book?
   (b) the length of your classroom?
   (c) the distance to the next town?
2. Measure:
   (a) the length and breadth of the pages of this book
   (b) the length of your classroom
   (c) compare your measurements with others in your group.
3. In a group, discuss:
   (a) how you would measure long distances like the distance from your school to your home.
   (b) how you would measure shorter distances such as the length and breadth of your classroom.
   (c) what problems there are about measuring distances that are not along a straight line.
   (d) ways of solving these problems.

The trundle wheel

Do you remember playing push the hoop? Thinking about that might help you with the ideas that follow.

There is a tool for measuring distances. It is called a trundle wheel. It is particularly useful for measuring distances along curves. Here are some ideas on how to make a trundle wheel.

Look at the picture of a trundle wheel. It is a wheel which turns on its axle. The axle is fixed to the handle so that a person can easily push the wheel along the ground. There is a mark on the rim (edge) of the wheel. To measure the distance from one point to another, start with the mark at the starting point on the ground. Push the wheel along, counting how many times it turns, until you come to the endpoint.

Suppose your wheel turns 200 times when you push it from point A to point B. If you know how far your wheel moves each time it turns, you will be able to calculate the distance between the two points. For example, if the wheel moves 0,6 metres for each revolution (complete turn), then in 200 revolutions it will go 200 x 0,6 = 120 metres.

How far would the wheel move in 200 revolutions if it moves n metres in one revolution?

Activity 3: Design and make a trundle wheel

Discuss these ideas in the group and then make a trundle wheel. Perhaps an old bicycle wheel may be useful, but if a bicycle wheel is not available you might think of using wire and something like an old tin lid. It is up to you and your group to decide what to use to make your trundle wheel. Do you think that the size of the wheel which you use to make your trundle wheel is important? What is the best size?

Before making your trundle wheel, all the groups must meet to discuss how they will be assessed. Are you only looking for accuracy or will you take into account their appearance, whether they have a counter for the number of turns which they make etc?

When you have finished, you will need to work out how far your wheel goes each time it turns around.
- Mark a point on the rim of the wheel.
- Draw a line on the ground and start with the mark on the wheel exactly on the line.
- Carefully roll the wheel in a straight line until the mark on its rim is again touching the ground.
- Mark that point on the ground.
- Use a ruler or tape measure to measure the distance between the two marks on the ground. That will tell you how far the wheel has moved.

Before measuring distances with your trundle wheel, discuss the following:
- What will happen if you lose count of the number of times the wheel turns? Can you invent something that will help you to count?
- Will your wheel turn easily – can you do anything to help it turn more easily?
- Does the wheel slip as it moves along?
- How important is it that the wheel should not slip?
- If it does slip, can you do anything to stop it from slipping?
- When you use it to measure a distance, will the wheel always turn an exact number of times? What can be done when there is not an exact number of turns?

Assessing the trundle wheels

Assess how accurately they measure distances and other criteria agreed upon.
To decide how accurately they measure distances,
- agree on a distance to be measured by all the groups and let your group measure it with your own trundle wheel.
- compare the results to see what differences there are between the measurements made by different groups. If there are differences, which wheel is the most accurate?
Why are there these differences?

Direction

You will know that the needle of a compass points North. Maps and plans usually show the northerly direction by means of an arrow.

Activity 4: Finding direction

1. (a) Find out where North is.
   (b) Point towards West.
   (c) How big is the angle between North and West?
   (d) Face the direction NW (North West) which is halfway between North and West
   (e) How many degrees is NW from north or from west?
   (f) Give the approximate direction of the police station from your school.

2. Go back to the map which you drew for your uncle and
   (a) draw an arrow which points North on the map.
   (b) write down the approximate direction from your home of two other places on your map.

3. (a) Mark a point on a piece of paper and draw arrows showing the directions N (North), S (South), E (East), W (West) and SW (South-west) from this point.
   (b) Do you know another way of writing SW using compass bearings?
   (c) Which of the two ways do you think is the better way to describe the direction which is halfway between South and West?

4. Make a copy of this diagram and then draw in arrows showing:

   (a) the direction SE of the clinic

   (b) the direction NW of the school.

5. Are you satisfied that the directions which you gave when answering questions 1(f) and 2(b) were accurate enough? If not, try to find out more about "bearings". Does anyone in your group understand what is meant by N 24° E?

Scale

Plans of buildings and also maps of cities, towns and roads, cannot be drawn full size. They are reduced in size (made smaller) but they have the same shape as the original. From the scale given, we are able to work out the actual size or distance. We call these maps and plans scale drawings.

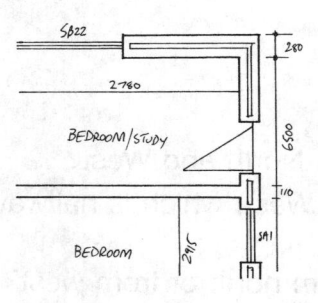

Activity 5: Using scale

The table below shows the length on a plan and the actual length on a building.

Length on plan (cm)	2	4	6	9		
Length of wall (m)	1	2			12	15

1. On your paper:
   (a) Complete the table.
   (b) Complete:
      (i) 2 cm on the plan represents ... m of the building

70

    (ii) 2 cm on the plan represents ... cm of the building

    (iii) 1 cm on the plan would represent ... cm of the building

From this we see that the scale = length on plan : actual building
$$= 2cm : 1m$$
$$= 2cm : 100cm$$
$$= 1 : 50$$

We say that the scale factor is 50 since any length on the building is ... times greater than that on the plan.

2. (a) Estimate (guess) the length and breadth of your classroom.

   (b) Measure the length and breadth of your classroom.

   (c) How good are you at estimating lengths?

   (d) Draw a plan of your classroom using a scale of 1 : 50

3. If a shop measures 20m x 55m and the plan of the shop measures 8cm x 22cm, work out the scale which has been used.

4. Using an atlas and your ruler:

   (a) measure the following as accurately as you can:

      (i) the shortest distance between Cape Town and Durban.

      (ii) the shortest distance to a place in another province which you would like to visit.

   (b) Use the scale given in your atlas to convert these to kilometres.

5. Here is part of a map showing some of the cities and towns.

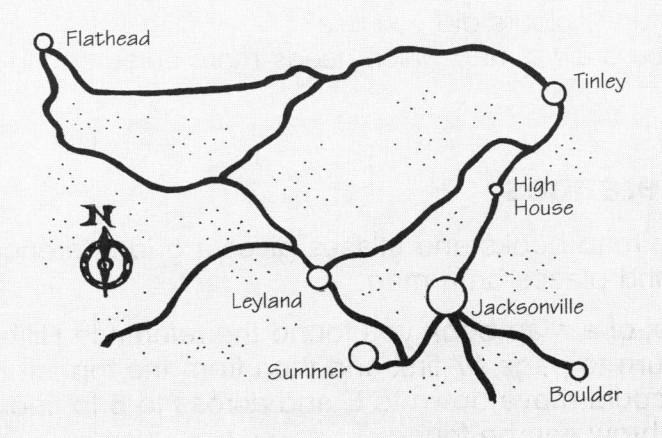

The scale of the map is 1 cm : 10 km.

(a) By measuring distances on the map, find the shortest distance between:
  (i) Summer and Tinley
  (ii) the 2 closest towns
  (ii) Summer and the town which is more or less NW of Summer.

(b) If a town is a distance of 200 km due East of Tinley, how far from Tinley must it be marked on the map?

(c) What scale factor was used?

6. In what way do you think that using a scale on your uncle's map might have been useful to him?

7. Can you think of other situations where scale is used? What people would use scale in their work?

PROBLEM SOLVER

Use as few colours as you can to colour all the separate areas of this map so that no two areas which share a common boundary (i.e. areas which are alongside each other) are coloured in the same colour.

Areas which only touch at a point may be the same colour.

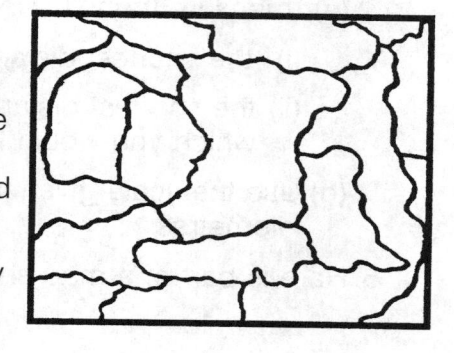

(a) How many colours did you use?
(b) Can you draw a map which needs more colours than this?

Grid References

The index to map books and atlases gives a grid reference to make it easier to find places on a map.

If in an index of a map book you found the reference Hillbrow 17 E5, you would turn to page 17 first and then from the top left hand corner you could move down to E and across to 5 to find the square in which Hillbrow can be found.

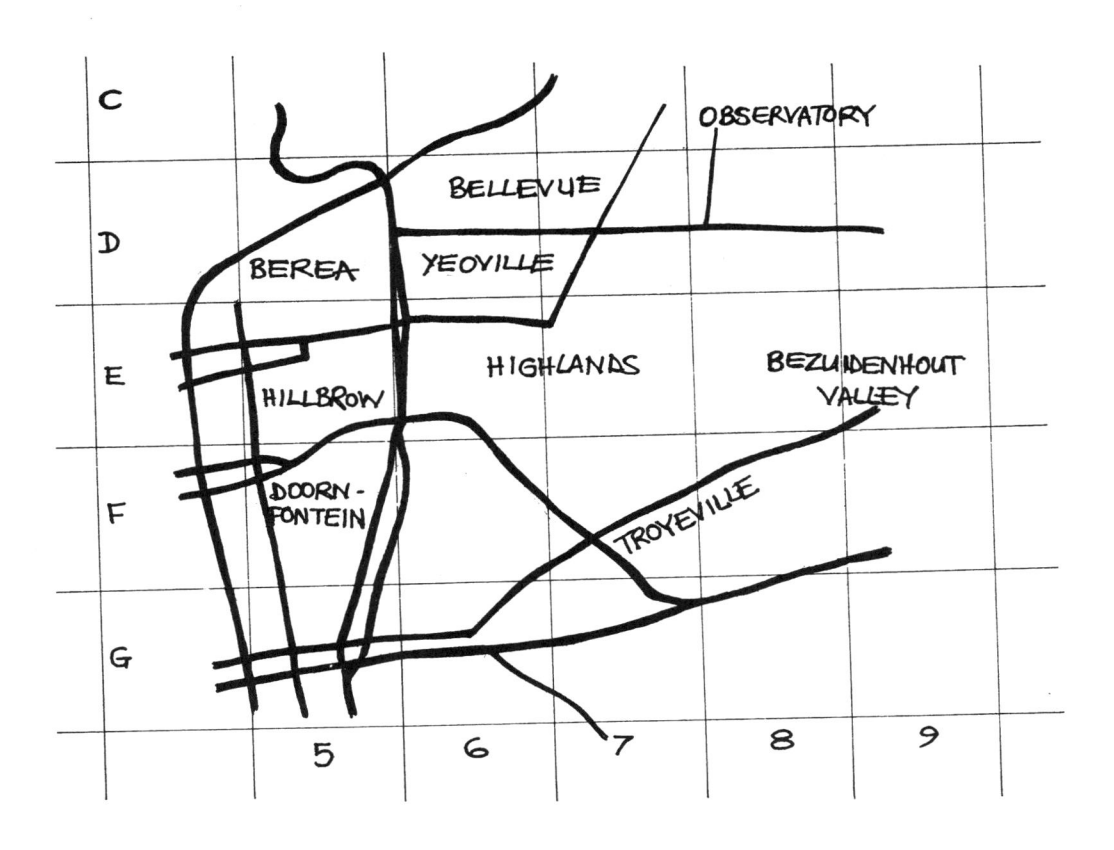

Activity 6: Using grid references

1. Using the map above, find the references which would appear in the index of the map book next to Yeoville, Observatory and Troyeville.
2. Add a grid reference to the map which you drew for your uncle and draw up an index to help him find the places which you marked on your map.
3. Find the town in which you live (or a town near to your home) in the index of your atlas and then use the given grid reference to find it on a map.
4. What are the advantages of having an index with grid references?

How did you do?

- Can you measure distances on the ground and on maps?
- Can you construct a trundle wheel and use it to measure distances?
- Can you use a map to find places and plan routes?
- Can you draw a map to find places and plan routes?
- Can you draw a map showing the position and distances of places from one another?
- Can you use the scale on a map to find the actual distance on the ground?
- Can you find north with or without using a compass?
- Are there any things in the unit which you still do not understand?

UNIT 8

Homes for All

For many years Blacks in this country were not allowed to own land. Many people did not have houses of their own. Much planning is now being done, and large sums of money are being spent on developing low-cost housing. One of the aims of the National Housing Policy is that all South Africans should be able to live in houses which will make their lives safer and will protect them from the weather. The policy aims to give people safe drinking water, adequate sanitation and electricity. When most new townships are planned and when older townships are improved, many people (including the community, the developer and the local authority) are consulted. For this reason it is important for people to have the skills and knowledge to get involved in meaningful ways.

In this unit you will have the opportunity to:
- understand simple scale plans
- use scale on a house plan to find actual distances
- draw your own scale plans
- construct a scale model of a house
- think about and discuss some of the issues that affect planning of a housing development

- experience some of the challenges facing both developers of new townships and the people who will live there
- solve problems and think creatively.

In a group discuss:

- Does low cost housing mean poor quality?
- What do you understand by adequate sanitation?
- When is water safe to drink?
- How can we make water safe to drink?
- Do you think it is right for local people to be consulted about housing? Why?

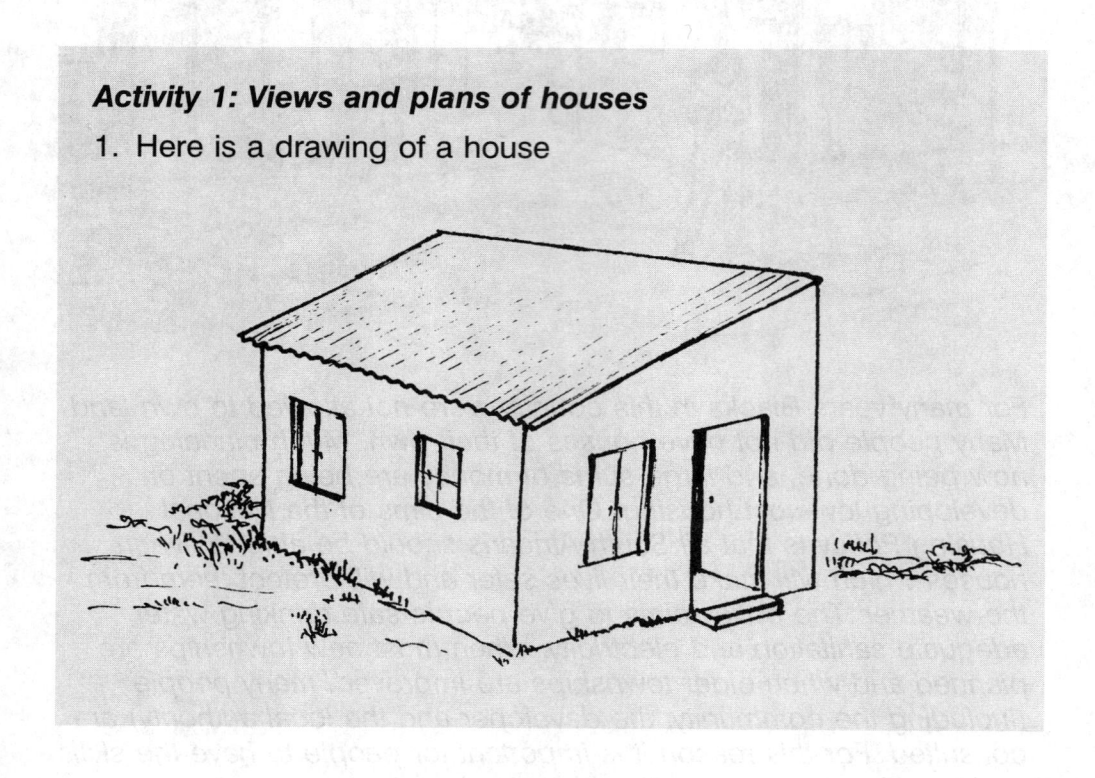

Activity 1: Views and plans of houses

1. Here is a drawing of a house

The view of one of the walls and the plan of the house are drawn below.

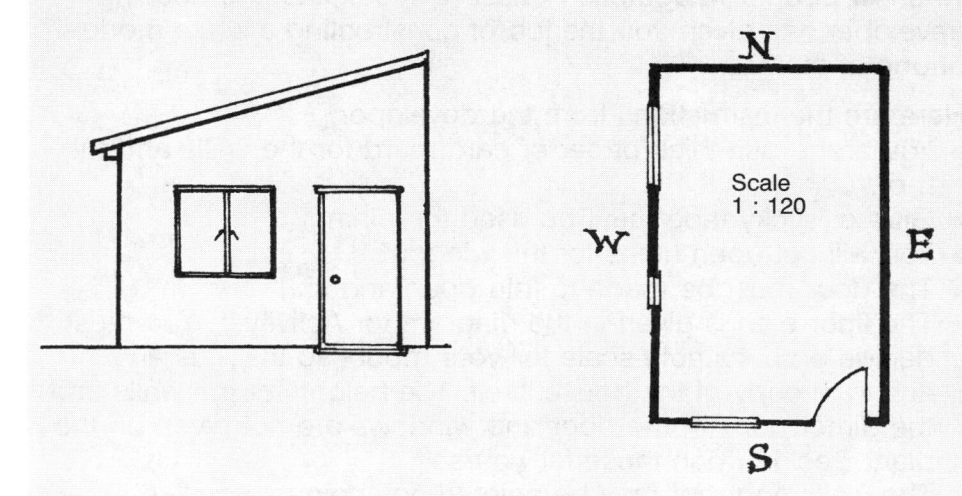

The house walls on the plan are labelled N, S, E and W according to the direction which they face. The scale used is shown on the plan.

(a) is the view which is drawn for you the N, S, E or W wall of the house?
(b) draw views of the other 3 walls.
(c) which two walls can be seen in the drawing of the house?
(d) from the plan, work out the length and breadth of the house and hence the area of the floor of the house.
(e) if the cost of building the house using concrete blocks is R8 226,99, work out the cost per square metre (to the nearest cent).
(f) redraw the plan on paper, and use dotted lines to design a room with an area of 15m^2 to be added to this house later.

2. (a) Suppose you are building a house using a plan with a scale of 1 : 40. Your plan shows a room which is 6 cm long. How long would you need to build the wall of the room?
(b) Suppose that you want to build a new room onto the side of the house, and want to change the existing plan. The length of one of the new walls is 2m. What length must you use on your plan?

Activity 2: Making a model of a house

To show people what these houses will look like, the housing developer has given you the job of constructing a scale model of one of them.

Here are the instructions from the developer:
- You are to use thick paper or cardboard for the walls and the roof.
- Glue or sticky tape must be used for joining.
- You will cut open holes for the windows.
- The door must be made to fold open and shut.
- The floor plan is given in the diagram for Activity 1. You must decide on a suitable scale for your model so that it is an accurate copy of the house itself. The heights of the walls and the dimensions of the door and windows are not given on the plan. Decide upon these for yourself.
- The walls and roof may be painted any colours you like.

1. With a partner make a model of the house in Activity 1.

2. When it is complete, discuss the following:
- Suppose you need to save glue or sticky tape. Are there ways of designing your model so that there will be fewer edges to stick together?
- The view of the house shows that it has a sloping roof. What are the disadvantages of a flat roof?

3. Compare your model with others before assessing your own. Things to look at are:
   (a) The slope of the roof
   - Whose model has the steepest roof?
   - How can you measure the steepness (slope) of a roof?
   - What steepness do you think is best for a house like this? Why?
   (b) How neat is your model?
   (c) Have you used colours and if so, do they improve the appearance of your model?
   (d) Does your model have anything special that the other models don't have?
   (e) Are there things about any of the other models that you particularly like?
   (f) Would you like to change your model in any way? If so, how?

Planning a housing development

Some of the issues to be negotiated when planning a housing development are the community facilities, individual housing units and the services needed. (Facilities are things like schools, clinics and sportsfields; services are things like sewers, electricity lines and water points.)

An urban area is in a city or town. Because less land is available in such areas, people have to live closer together. This is known as a high density population area. Housing developments take place in high or low density urban or rural areas.

Tell your partner what you understand by a low density rural area.

Activity 3: Planning a housing development

A high density, low cost development is planned in a certain urban region of KwaZulu-Natal.

The table below gives a rough guide to the size of the facility, the number of houses that can be served by each facility, and how far from houses the facility should be.

Facility	Number of houses per facility	Maximum distance from houses	Size of land
Creche	300	300 metres	0,1 ha
Primary School	500	700 metres	0,7 - 1,4 ha
Secondary School	1 500	1 400 metres	1,4 - 2,6 ha
Sportsfield	1 per secondary school and 1 for every 2 primary schools		0,65 ha

1. In your group, discuss the questions that follow. Remember that the table gives recommendations for a high density urban area. There are no right or wrong answers to the questions.
   (a) What is meant by a high density urban area?
   (b) Why do you think that the suggested number of houses that a primary school should serve is so much less than that of a secondary school? Is it a good suggestion?
   (c) (i) What is the greatest distance that anyone in your group has to travel from home to school?
   (ii) What is the average distance from school to home of learners in your group? How does the average compare with what is recommended in this report? Discuss the recommendation.

(iii) Carry out a survey of all the learners in your class to find out whether the primary school which they went to was closer to their home than their secondary school.

(d) The area of large pieces of land is given in hectares.
1 ha = 10 000 m^2.
Using figures in the table above, work out the number of square metres each of the facilities would cover.

(e) By pacing out, work out the approximate area of land that your school covers.

(f) What are the most popular school sports? What are the dimensions of fields that are needed to play these sports? Using a suitable scale, plan the use of a sportsfield which covers 0,65 ha.

(g) What other facilities do you think should be provided for when planning a housing development?

2. The recommended size of plots in the above housing development was between 200 and 400 square metres.

(a) In the school grounds, pace out two different rectangular plots of land: one that covers 200 m^2 and one that covers 400m^2. What was the length and breadth of each plot? Compare the dimensions of your plots with those of other groups.

(b) Do you think that it is important that the piece of land should be rectangular? Explain.

(c) A government report in 1999 stated that almost 200 000 homes need to be built each year to keep up with the growth of the South African population. Do you think that the same size plots would be allocated in a high density growth area such as Gauteng as in a low density area such as Northern Province? Explain.

(d) Estimate how big the piece of land is on which your house is built. Pace it out when you get home.

Activity 4: Planning a high density low cost development

Suppose you live in a high density area where there is a need to build 3 500 new low cost houses.

A rectangular piece of land with a length of 2 500 metres and a breadth of 800 metres covering an area of 200 hectares has been set aside for the development. Your group has been elected by the community to represent them in negotiations between the developer and the local authority. Your first task is to meet with the community to talk about community needs. As a group, discuss the following issues and decide upon recommendations which you would like to make to the developer.

1. Services are commodities like water, sewerage and rubbish removal, roads and electricity.
   What factors do you think will influence the services offered?

Some things to be considered in your planning are:
- will each house have its own water supply or will a number of houses share a standpipe?
- will no roads, all roads or only the main bus and taxi routes be tarred?
- will there be pit latrines, septic tanks or main-line sewerage?

2. Draw up a table like the one below (adding other facilities) to show how much land is needed altogether and for what purpose it will be used. Remember that you only have 200 hectares of land available. Do not forget to allow for roads.

	Number	Size of each	Total area required
Houses	3 500		
Secondary schools			

PROBLEM SOLVER

There are 100 houses numbered from 1 to 100 along one of the roads in this development. The developer has a box of single digits from which he is going to make up all the numbers for the houses. How many of each digit does he need?
(Hint: To number house 51 he will use two digits, a 5 and a 1 and to number house 32, he will use a 3 and a 2 etc).

Activity 5: Street Plans

When a township is planned, the layout of roads is very important. Sometimes, straight roads are laid out in a grid system like in the diagram. In many townships, this is not the case. Roads are often not straight and often they are not laid out in a grid. It is easy to arrange rectangular plots of land on a grid system with straight roads. Discuss in a group:

1. Are there other advantages to having the roads in a grid like in the diagram above?
   (Think of advantages to the township developers as well as to the people who live in the houses.)
2. Does the straight line grid system have disadvantages?
3. What things do you think would affect the layout of roads in a new township?

INVESTIGATE ■□■□■□■□■□

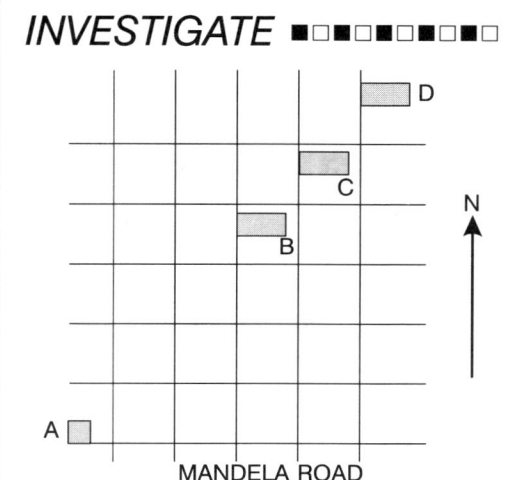

Here is a road map of part of the township where Vusi lives. He lives in the house A on Mandela Rd. The plot is fenced with a gate onto Mandela Rd. There is a school at B. Every day Vusi walks along the streets on his way to the school. He does not take any short cuts across other people's land.

Vusi's sister asked him one day. "What is your shortest route to school?"

"There are many" said Vusi.

Discuss with a partner:

1. What does Vusi mean? Is he correct?
2. Assuming that Vusi always walks in either a northerly or an easterly direction, in how many different ways can he get to school along the streets?
3. Are they all the same distance?
4. If you were Vusi, what things would help you decide which way to walk to school?
5. How many different routes are there from Vusi's home to the Post Office at C?
6. And to the shebeen at D?
7. What general pattern or rule comes from these examples? Try to write it down in words or mathematical symbols.

How did you do?

- Can you make a floor plan of a building using a suitable scale?
- Can you make a model of a house from a drawing and a plan?
- Can you find the actual length of a wall of a building from a plan?
- Can you convert areas from hectares to square metres?
- Do you have some idea of the area needed to build schools, houses etc?
- Do you understand some of the ways in which a community can be involved in planning a housing development?

UNIT 9

A Collection of Containers

Our world is made up of solid objects. Every object that we can see has three dimensions; a height, a width and a depth. Some everyday examples are: a box of cereal, a can of coke, a table. Look at the picture above and around your classroom and find some more examples.

The ancient Greeks had a particular interest in the study of solid shapes and their word polyhedron is used to describe a solid figure with 4 or more flat surfaces.

What do you think poly means?

Can you think of any other terms beginning with poly?

In this unit you will be exposed to:

- finding the surface area of 3-dimensional shapes by using nets
- using nets to build various 3-dimensional shapes like boxes or cylinders
- finding the volume (the space that the 3-dimensional shape takes up) of various objects
- the difference between weight and mass
- the meaning of density
- applying formulae to calculate volume and density.

Activity 1: Design and make creative containers

You and your friends decide to start your own business. You want to make gift boxes, decorate them, fill them with different contents like sweets or soap or pencils and then sell them. These are the containers that you would like to make.

Below are the nets (the unfolded flat shape of the container) of some 3-dimensional shapes.

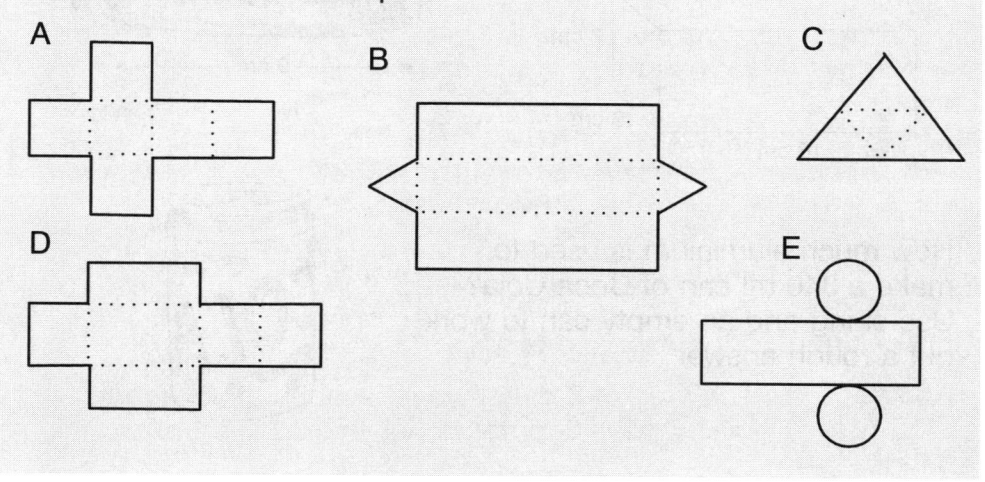

A

B

C

D

E

85

1. Can you match the correct net with its container on pages 84 and 85?
2. Using cardboard, scissors, tape and glue, use the nets to make all the containers to your own measurements.
3. Calculate the area of each face (flat side) of the different containers.
4. Calculate the total surface area of each container.
5. Can you work out a rule or formula for finding the surface area?
6. Can you match the following mathematical names of polyhedra with the containers on the previous page?

   (a) rectangular prism   (b) cylinder   (c) pyramid
   (d) cube   (e) triangular prism

Exercise 1

Find the surface area of the following:

1. 18 cm, 9 cm, 7 cm

2. 9 cm, 4,5 cm

3. How much aluminium is used to make a 340 ml can of Coca Cola? Use string and an empty can to work out a rough answer.

INVESTIGATE ■□■□■□■□■□

Let us take the shape of the rectangular prism.

A.

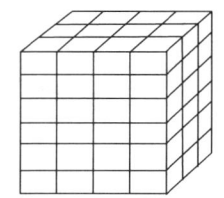

B.

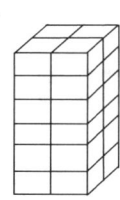

1. How many blocks are there on the bottom layer of A?
2. What is a quick way to work the answer out?
3. How many blocks high is the prism?
4. How many blocks are there altogether?
5. Can you work out a rule to find out the volume using the area of the base and the height?
   See if your rule works for B
6. If each block is a cube with each side measuring 1 cm, what is the volume of B in cm^3?

You have probably worked out that volume of a rectangular prism is length x breadth x height or area of the base x height. The formula, Volume = area of base x height can be used to find the volume of triangular and cylindrical prisms.

Example. Find the volume of the following:

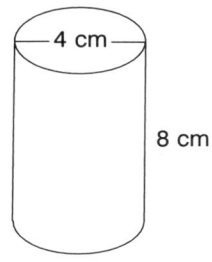

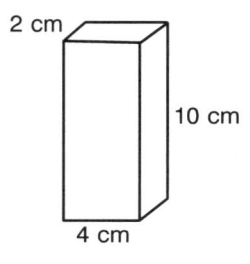

1. volume of cylinder
   = area of base × height
   = area of circle × height
   = π × radius^2 × height
   = 3,14 × (2)^2 × 8
   = 100,48 cm^3

2. volume of rectangular prism
   = area of base × height
   = area of rectangle × height
   = 2 × 4 × 10 cm^3
   = 80 cm^3

Exercise 2

Suppose these are 3 containers that you have made. Find their volumes (in cm^3).

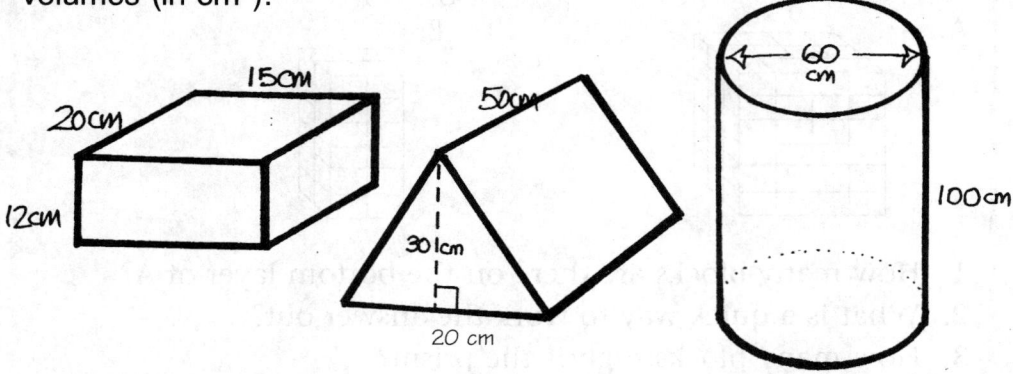

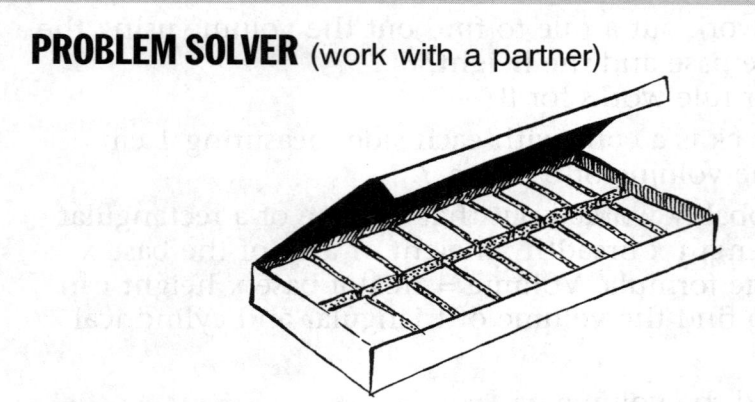

Container 1 (rectangular box): 20 cm, 15 cm, 12 cm

Container 2 (triangular prism): 50 cm long, triangle base 20 cm, height 30 cm

Container 3 (cylinder): diameter 60 cm, height 100 cm

PROBLEM SOLVER (work with a partner)

You decide to fill your rectangular box with home made chocolate. Each piece of chocolate is 2 cm thick and cut into shapes 3 cm by 2 cm.

1. If you pack 18 pieces of chocolate into your container, what will the volume of the container be?
2. Work out the dimensions (measurements) of a box that your chocolate will fit into exactly.
3. Is there only one possible answer?
4. How many different answers could you have? Sketch some possible containers showing their dimensions.
5. Is the surface area of each container the same?
6. Which measurements produce the cheapest box to make?
7. Which measurements produce a box which you feel is the best container for your product?

Activity 2: Mr Moosa's shed

Mr. Moosa has a shed on his smallholding. He decides to paint the outside walls, door and roof.

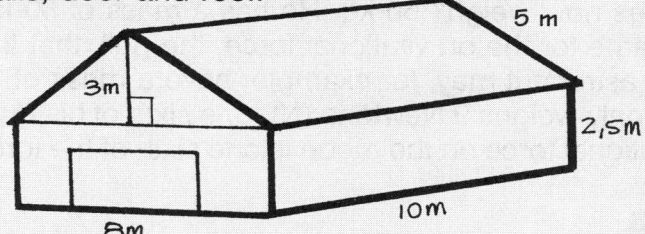

1. Calculate the total surface area of the exterior (outside) of the shed.
2. Draw a net of the shed, using a scale of 1m : 1cm.
3. Using a scale of 1m : 1 cm, build a model of the shed
4. If he was able to paint 5m^2 for every litre of paint, how many litres of paint does he need to paint the outside of the shed?
5. The cost of the paint is R210,00 for 25 litres. Calculate the cost of painting the shed.
6. The shed is being used to store bales of straw.
   Each straw bale measures 1m x 0,5m x 0,5m.
   What is the volume of one bale of straw?
7. If Mr. Moosa packs the straw bales to a height of 3m, how many layers of bales can he pack? 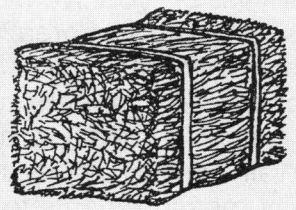
8. What volume of straw can be stored in the shed if he keeps a 3m x 3m area open inside the shed?
9. Behind the shed is a cylindrical water tank that has a radius of 3m and is 2m high.
   What is the volume of the water tank?
10. If 1 litre = 1000cm^3, how many litres of water can the tank hold?  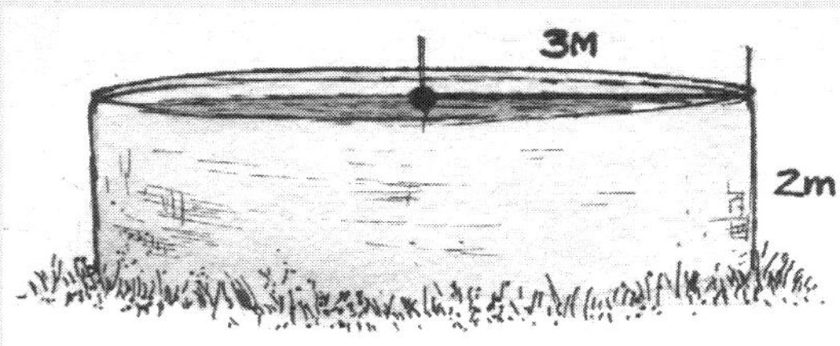
11. Because of the drought the water tank is only $\frac{1}{2}$ full. How many litres of water are in the tank?

Mass and Weight

People often use the word "weight" when they really mean "mass". A man does not "weigh" 50 kg. He has a mass of 50 kg. Weight is another name for the gravitational force, the pull, that the earth has on us. An astronaut may, for example, have a mass of 54 kg. On the moon, he only weighs 9 Newtons (N), one sixth of his mass, because the gravitational force on the moon is one sixth of the force on earth.

Exercise 3
1. What is your mass?
2. What would your mass be if you were on the moon?
3. What would your weight be on the moon?

Density

What do you think is meant by density?
Population density is defined as the average number of people living on a given area of land. It is used to show how crowded a city or country is. Do you live in a densely populated (crowded) area or a sparsely populated area?
The scientific definition of density is the mass of an object divided by its volume, that is, density = mass ÷ volume.
Who needs to measure density? Airline pilots, for example, need to know air density before they take off. Geologists, for example, use density measurements to identify types of rock.

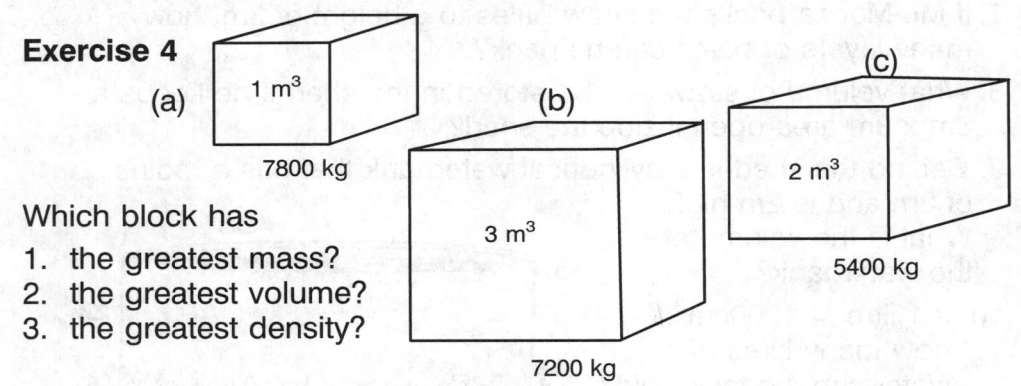

Exercise 4

(a) 1 m^3, 7800 kg

(b) 3 m^3, 7200 kg

(c) 2 m^3, 5400 kg

Which block has
1. the greatest mass?
2. the greatest volume?
3. the greatest density?

Activity 3: Which has the greater density, cream or milk?

Fill a small container with milk. Record its mass.
Fill the container with cream. Record its mass.
Were you surprised to find that cream is less dense than milk?
This is why cream always rises to the top of the milk.

PROBLEM SOLVER

1. Can you explain why ice floats on water?

2. A builder wants to lift a load of 80 solid concrete blocks on his lorry. The load measures 2m x 2m x 0.5m.

Work out:
a) the volume of the concrete
b) the mass of the concrete, if the density of concrete is 2400kg/m^3
c) whether he can safely carry all the blocks on the lorry, if the maximum load is 3000kg and if not, how many blocks he can carry.

Displacement

How do we find the volume of a strangely shaped object, for example, your hand?

Activity 4: (You need a jar of water, big enough to fit your hand in, a shallow dish to stand the jar in and a measuring jug in ml).

1. Place the jar in the shallow dish and fill it to the top with water.
2. Gently lower your hand into the water up to your wrist. Water will be displaced and overflow into the dish.
3. Pour the displaced water out of the dish into the measuring jug. Read how many ml were displaced by your hand.
4. Calculate the volume of your hand (1 ml = 1 cm^3).

How did you do?

- Are you able to calculate the surface area and volume of different objects?
- Were you able to construct the containers?
- Which part of this unit did you find interesting?
- Which part did you find the most difficult?

UNIT 10

Running A Car

Transport is really necessary for all of us, whether it is our own or public transport. A large amount of the money that we earn is spent on just getting to work or school and then home again. What do you think is going on in this picture? What is the man thinking to himself? Is it easy to see from the diagram? We also spend a lot of time in cars or buses without even considering how much we rely on transport. Which form of transport gets people to their destination fastest? Give some reasons why you chose the one that you did.

In this unit you will be given the opportunity to:
- discuss what is the best type of transport to use and how to decide this
- analyse bar graphs, pie charts, broken line graphs and distance-time graphs
- extract data from a table and see how it applies in a real life situation
- work out a family budget
- work out speed from a graph
- convert speed in km/h to other units.

Decision making

One of the first decisions that you will have to make when you leave school is the sort of transport that you are going to use

INVESTIGATE ■□■□■□■□■□

In groups of 4 to 6 people, discuss whether you should:

(a) buy a bicycle

(b) buy a motorbike

(c) buy a second hand car

(d) buy a new car

(e) use the local bus service

(f) use the local taxi service.

To gather information for your discussion, interview different people, for example teachers with cars, people who may use buses/taxis, people who ride bicycles or motorbikes. Ask them to tell you about their petrol costs; running costs; repayment and so on.

In your discussion you should talk about
- safety—how safe is each option?
- cost—how much money you earn and how much you can afford to spend on transport
- running costs (if you decide to buy)—petrol, services etc.
- anything else that helps you make a decision.

Discuss the sort of transport that different people use:
- What would a student use?
- What would a doctor use?
- What would a self-employed person use?
- Present the decision of your group to the class by using a chart and having a report back session.

Financing the car

There are no right or wrong answers to this question about what is the best sort of transport to use. We are now going to assume that you have decided to buy a car. Most people do not have the amount of cash needed to buy a car, so they borrow money from a bank. This is called *financing the car*. Of course, when you borrow money, you have to pay interest on the money that you have borrowed. Interest is the extra money that you pay back to the bank as a charge for borrowing money from them.

Let's say you have decided that you can afford to spend R20 000 on a second hand car, but that you only have R4 000 saved up. A finance institution (bank) agrees to lend you the balance of the money, which you will pay back with interest.

Activity 1: What car should I buy

In groups of two: Look in some recent newspapers and try to identify some cars that *you* would buy if you had R20 000 to spend on a car. Look at cars that fall into the following categories: small or large; older or newer; car or bakkie. Ask people who have similar cars to the one that you are thinking about buying about their petrol costs. What is the price of petrol per litre? How much would it cost to fill a 40 litre tank? How much would it cost to fill a 65 litre tank? Make a chart that lists the pros and cons of each car.

We can use a formula to find out how much interest you will pay on the R20 000 that you have borrowed from the bank. This type of interest is called compound interest. Try to find out the difference between compound interest and simple interest.

Amount borrowed	Annual interest rate paid	Number of years to repay	Amount paid	Payment per month	Interest paid overall
16 000	16%	3	R20 250,45	R562,51	R4 250,45
16 000	16%	4	R21 765,34	R453,44	R5 765,34
16 000	16%	5	R23 345,33	R389,09	R7 345,33

Graph no. 1
How amount paid in total changes as the number of years to repay the loan changes

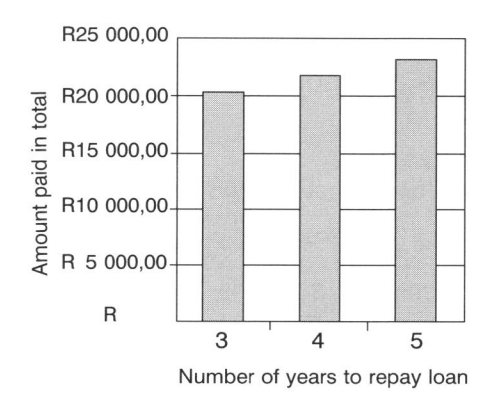

Graph no. 2
How your repayment changes as you take longer to repay the loan

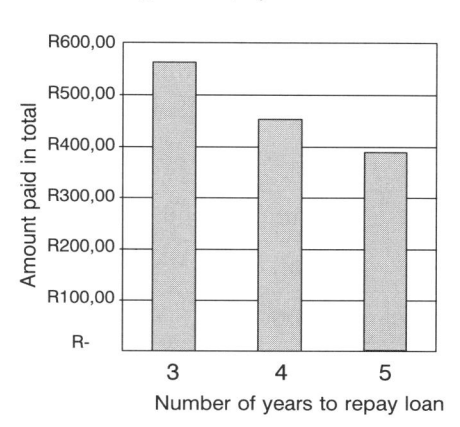

Exercise 1

Answer the following questions using the above graphs and the table.

1. What is graph no. 1 trying to show you?
2. Why is the total amount of money repaid over 5 years so much more than the amount of money repaid over 3 years?
3. What is graph no. 2 trying to show you?
4. Why is the amount of money paid per month over 5 years less than the amount of money paid per month over 3 years?
5. Which option is best—to repay your loan over 3, 4 or 5 years? Why?

6. How do you think graph no. 1 will change if R20 000 is borrowed? Why?
7. How will graph no. 1 change if R10 000 is borrowed? Why?
8. What do you think will happen to graph no. 2 if the interest rate changes from 16% to 18%?
9. What do you think will happen to graph no. 2 if the interest rate decreases?

Running costs

The actual payment of the car is not the only major expense in owning a car. The running costs that you have to consider when you own a car are also important. These running costs include things like the cost of petrol, repairs, services and general wear and tear on the car.

	Budgeted monthly running costs for the first year (in Rands)												
	Jan	Feb	Mar	Apr.	May	Jun	Jul	Aug	Sept	Oct	Nov	Dec	
petrol	300	300	300	300	300	300	300	300	300	300	300	300	3600
services	500												500
tyres							500						500
licence	120												120
repayments	390	390	390	390	390	390	390	390	390	390	390	390	4680
insurance	200	200	200	200	200	200	200	200	200	200	200	200	2400
Total	1510	890	890	890	890	890	1390	890	890	890	890	890	R11 800

Activity 2: How much do I budget?

In pairs discuss how someone decides on what amount to budget (expect to spend) for each of the items or commodities in the table above. How would you check to make sure that your budgeted costs are realistic? What would happen if your *actual* costs were lower or higher than the budgeted costs? Give some examples where you think the budgeted and actual costs could be different.

Exercise 2

Pie Chart

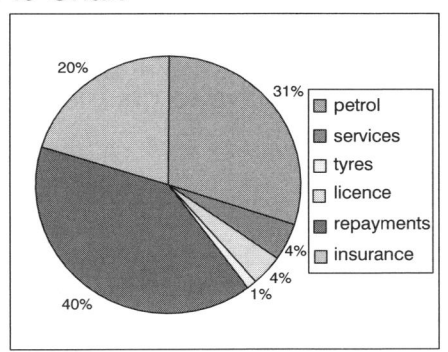

Bar graph

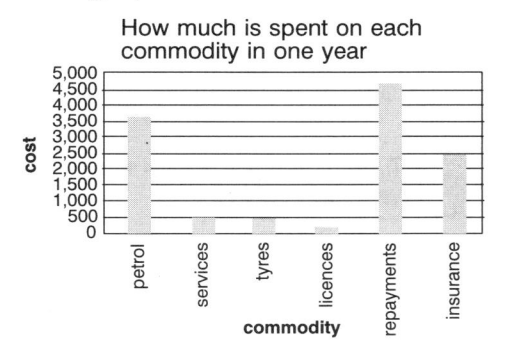

How much is spent on each commodity in one year

The pie chart shows the percentages of each of the budgeted expenses in running a car. The bar graph shows how much money is spent on each commodity in one year. Answer the following questions:
1. What takes up most of the money in owning a car?
2. What takes up the least amount of money?
3. Do you think that the amount of money spent on petrol per month is realistic? If not, then what should it be?
4. What does the pie chart tell you?
5. What can you read off the bar graph? Why is it not as useful as the pie chart?

INVESTIGATE ■□■□■□■□

You have been asked to help two family members draw up budgets for their expenses to show how the family income will be spent over a one year period.

Uncle John earns R8 050 per month and he has 2 children aged 14 and 12. His wife and mother live with him.

Your grandmother lives with your grandfather. Your grandfather gets a pension of R850 and your grandmother gets a state pension of R501 per month.

You must — first decide what the expenses of each family are
— draw up a table to show the expenses from January to December
— represent the expenses using either a bar graph, a pie chart or a broken line graph.

Travelling in a car
Distance and displacement

Whenever we get in a car, we think of how fast we are going to travel, how far we have to go, and how long we have to get there.

Look at this diagram of a journey to school. We leave home, go to school, then after school stop at the shop before going home again. Lets say that the school is 4km from your home, the shop is 2km from the school and your home is 3km from the shop.

Exercise 3

1. When you get to school how far are you away from home?
2. When you get to the shop, how far are you from home?
3. When you get back home again, how far have you travelled altogether? How far are you away from where you started before you left home?
4. If you go to school and then straight home again, what distance have you travelled? How far are you away from where you started before you left home?
5. If you go to the shop and then home again, what distance have you travelled? How far are you away from where you started before you left home?

The distance altogether that you have travelled when you return home after going to school, the shop and then back home, is 9km. But your displacement from home at the end of the day is 0km. How is this so? Well, displacement is how far you are at the end from where you started. If you started at home and ended at home, then your displacement is 0. Distance is how far you have physically travelled.

Distance, time and speed

When we consider the motion of an object, how far the object moves is important, but so is how long the object takes to go a certain distance. The object can be a person, a car, a bus, or the moon around the sun, or anything that can move. The motion is how fast or slow it is moving, or if it is moving at a constant speed or accelerating. We will talk about the motion of a car driving along a road, and a person walking or running.

How to read a graph:

1. Look at how the axes are labelled (what it says up the side and the numbers, and what it says underneath and the numbers).
2. Going up is called the vertical or y-axis.
3. Underneath is called the horizontal, or x-axis.

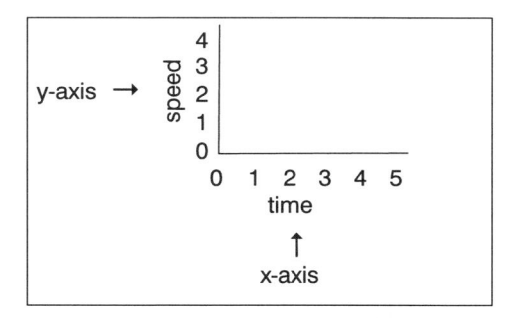

On the three graphs that follow, distance is on the y-axis and time is on the x-axis.

The first graph shows distance in kilometres on the y-axis and time in hours on the x-axis. This means that the graph tells us how distance in kilometres (km) changes as hours (h) pass. This is speed, measured in kilometres per hour (km/h).

In Graph 1 below

At point A, the object (lets say it is a car) has not yet moved.

At point B, the car has moved 200 km and it has taken 3 hours to do that.

At point C, 2 hours have passed but the car has not moved any further. In other words, it is stationary.

At point D, the car has moved 300 km and has taken a further 5 hours to do this.

Exercise 4. Graph 1

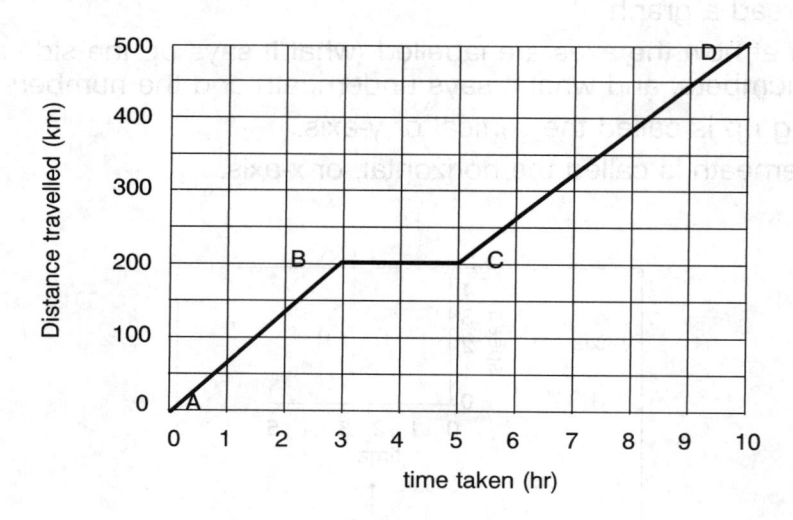

1. What speed did the car travel between points A and B?
2. What speed did the car travel between points B and C?
3. What speed did the car travel between points C and D?

To find speed, you should have worked out how far the car has moved by looking at the y-axis, and divided by how much time has passed, by looking at the x-axis.

Exercise 5. Graph 2

1. What is measured on the y-axis (give the units as well)?
2. What is measured on the x-axis (give the units as well)?
3. What is the speed of the object between A and B?
4. What is the speed of the object between B and C?
5. What is the speed of the object between C and D?
6. Do you think this graph is representing a journey by car, bicycle or on foot?

Exercise 6. Graph 3

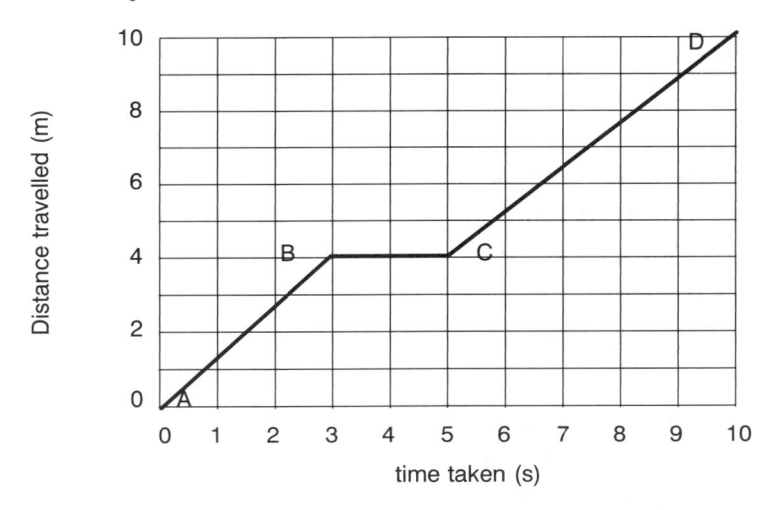

1. What is measured on the y-axis (give the units as well)?
2. What is measured on the x-axis (give the units as well)?
3. What is the speed of the object between A and B?

4. What is the speed of the object between B and C?
5. What is the speed of the object between C and D?
6. Do you think this graph is representing a journey by car, bicycle or on foot?

Converting kilometres per hour to metres per second

Graph 1 shows distance in km and time in h, so that the speed from this graph will be in km/h. We cannot compare this speed to the speed from graphs 2 and 3 because they show speed in km/min and m/s. We need to be able to convert speed from one unit to another so that we can compare different speeds.

To convert: km/h to m/s: $\times \frac{1000}{3600}$

eg. 60 km/h = 60 $\times \frac{1000}{3600}$ = 16,67 m/s

To convert: km/min to m/s: $\times \frac{1000}{60}$

eg. 0,13 km/min = 0,13 $\times \frac{1000}{60}$ = 2,22 m/s

To convert: m/s to km/h: $\times \frac{3600}{1000}$

eg. 20 m/s = 20 $\times \frac{3600}{1000}$ = 72 km/h

To convert: km/h to km/min: $\times \frac{1}{60}$

eg. 11 km/h = 11 $\times \frac{1}{60}$ = 0,18 km/min.

Exercise 7
1. Convert 100 km/h to m/s.
2. Convert 4 km/h to km/min.
3. Convert 20 m/s to km/h.
4. Convert 0,1 km/min to m/s.
5. You enter a walking race and it takes you 55 minutes to complete the 7 km.
   (a) What is your speed in km/h?
   (b) The winners run this race and they run at a speed of 3,5 minutes per kilometre.
   How many minutes did it take the winner to run the race?

(c) What was his speed in km/h and in m/s?
The cut off time for the race is $1\frac{1}{2}$ hours.

(d) What is the slowest speed (in km/h and m/s) that someone can walk at and still make it to the finish in time?

PROBLEM SOLVER

You travel from Durban to Pietermaritzburg (which is exactly 100km) at 100km/h and back at 200km/h. What is your average speed?

How did you do?

- Could you explain clearly why you chose the method of transport that you did in the first discussion?
- Did you manage to work out a budget for your grandparents and your uncle?
- Could you display it using a chart?
- Did you understand the difference between distance and displacement?
- Could you work out speed from the three graphs?
- Could you manage the conversions of speed from one unit to another?
- Which section did you find the most interesting?
- Which section do you think is the most useful for you?
- Is there any part of this unit that still bothers you? Why?

UNIT 11

Money, money, money

Sales Representative:
Urgently required. Own car essential.
Commission only.

Assistant Accountant:
Excellent salary. To start immediately.

Part-time Cashiers:
R10 per hour.

Mechanic required:
Wages R500 per week.

Management consultant:
Required to give advice to business.
R50 000 for task.

The above adverts show how different jobs are paid. Some people get paid hourly, some get paid weekly, others get paid monthly, some are paid commission only (which means they only get paid a certain percentage of what they sell) and others get paid for doing a particular job.

In this unit you will

- investigate different types of professions and how people are paid
- learn how to calculate commission
- look at the difference between earnings and take home pay
- calculate payment of tax
- discuss how to manage your money by cutting down on costs
- work out simple interest
- look at exchange rates and travel.

Activity 1: What sort of job?

In pairs, find out about the following jobs in the list below. Find out what each person does, what qualifications are required to do the job and how the person is generally paid (is the person paid hourly, weekly, monthly or commission only?). See how many jobs you can add to the list (the list can be very long).

Then select the type of job you would like to do and report back on your reasons for choosing such a job.

Possible jobs:

Factory worker	Farm worker	Cashier
Banker	Teacher	Financial Adviser
Builder	Computer Technician	Labourer
Computer Programmer	Business Owner	Technician
Representative	Engineer	Lawyer
Insurance Salesman	Consultant	Estate Agent
Politician	Gardener	TV Technician
Nurse	TV Announcer	Doctor
Journalist	Cleaner	Accountant
Security Guard	Traffic Official	Policeman
Army Officer	Chef	Farmer

Exercise 1

1. How much does a person working 5 hours a day at a rate of R8,75 per hour earn in one day?
2. If that person works for 23 days, how much does he earn?
3. A person earns R15 an hour and works for 8 hours a day and 5 days a week. Another person earns R600 per week. Who earns the most?
4. A carpenter is paid R25 per chair made. If the carpenter completed 26 chairs, how much was the carpenter paid?
5. A salesperson earns R200 plus 10% of the value of the sale. If she sold R3 000 worth of goods, what did she earn?
6. A manager earned R40 000 in her first year. What were her weekly earnings?
7. If the manager's salary rose by R2 000 per year, how many years will it take to reach the maximum salary of R56 000?

Commission

Commission is generally earned by salespersons. They sometimes do not receive any basic salary but only earn a certain percentage commission on the sales that they make. (Percentage means out of 100, so 15% is 15 out of 100 or $\frac{15}{100}$).

So a person who earns commission of 10% on a sale of R40 000 will make: 10% of R40 000

10% of R40 000

$= \frac{10}{100} \times 40\ 000$

$= \frac{1}{10} \times 40\ 000$

$= R4000.$

Exercise 2
1. A sales representative gets 7% commission on sales of R70 000. What does he earn?
2. An estate agent earns 3% commission on the sale of a house valued at R200 000. What commission does the estate agent earn?
3. Which is the larger amount: 6% of R50 000 or 8% of R40 000?
4. A sales representative earns 5% commission on sales up to R50 000 and 7% on sales above R50 000. If the sales representative made sales of R65 000, what commission did she earn?

Take-home income

If you are an **employee** (employed by someone else) then you will be paid a monthly salary or weekly wage. Your **employer** will take money for UIF (unemployment insurance), medical aid, tax and pension off your salary. This money is called deductions. The money that is left is your Take-home income.

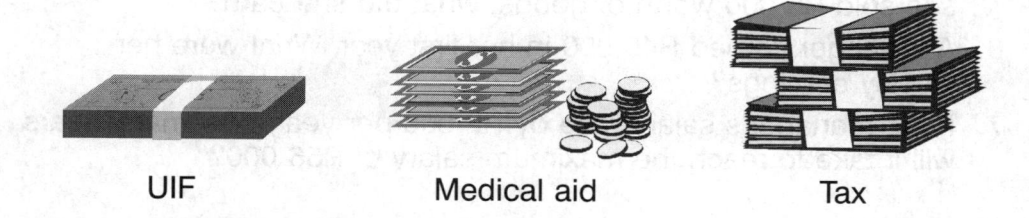

UIF   Medical aid   Tax

Tax

All people in South Africa who earn money pay taxes if their earnings are greater than a certain amount. Generally, the more a person earns, the more tax that person pays. The government uses the money collected from taxes to pay Civil Servants (people employed by the government including politicians, police, the army, teachers and others) and to build schools, hospitals, roads and other facilities needed by the population.

The government has worked out tax tables from which it is possible to see the amount of tax a person must pay.

Tax rates for individuals

Taxable income	Rates of tax
Less than R31 000 per year	19% of earnings
More than R31 000 up to R46 000	R5 890 plus 30% on all earnings greater than R31000
More than R46 000 up to R60 000	R10 390 plus 39% on all earnings greater than R46 000
More than R60 000 up to R70 000	R15 850 plus 43% on all earnings greater than R60 000
More than R70 000 up to R120 000	R20 150 plus 44% on all earnings greater than R70 000
More than R120 000	R42 150 plus 45% on all earnings greater than R120 000

Let us work out the tax of a person earning R50 000 per year:

R50 000 is between R46 000 and R60 000. So the person pays R10 390 plus 39% on (R50 000 − R46 000) = R4 000.

39% of R4 000 = $\frac{39}{100}$ × 4000 = 39 × 40 = R1 560

Hence the person pays R10 390 + R1 560 = R11 950 tax per year.

Exercise 3
1. Work out 30% of R180.
2. Work out 35% of R40 000.
3. Work out what someone who earns R31 000 per year pays in tax.
4. Work out what someone who earns R80 000 per year pays in tax.
5. Work out the difference in tax between someone who earns R70 000 per year and someone who earns R72 000 per year.

Activity 2: More taxes

There are many other forms of taxes that the government uses to collect money, other than direct tax on income (income tax). In groups find out what other forms of tax there are.

Managing your money: Spending

You will need to draw up a budget to check where your money goes:

Nkosinathi has R500 take-home income per week:
He wants to buy a car which will cost him R150 per week.
His expenses are as follows:

Expense:	Amount:
Rent	R150
Food	R100
Bus fare	R40
Clothing account	R20
Entertainment	R50
Savings	R50
Total:	___

Can he afford to buy the car? His food expenses include R30 a week on fast food at various take-aways.

What can he do to make sure he can buy the car?

Exercise 4

1. Thandi decides to make a dress for herself. The pattern cost R5, the material cost R15,50, the cotton cost R2,30 and the buttons cost R1,40.
   (a) What was the cost of making the dress?
   (b) What did she save if a similar dress is priced R70,99 in the shop?
2. Three friends decide to buy two hamburgers and share them. One cost R9,20 and the other R12,50.
   (a) What was the total cost?
   (b) How much should each person pay?
3. Crazy Paving Company told Mr Mkhize that they could pave his driveway for R5 000. He decided to do it himself and bought 255 paving stones at R15 each. The delivery charge for the paving stones was R300. How much money did he save himself?
4. Mrs Ngubane has take-home weekly wage of R450. She pays rent of R55 for a flat and is paying off a car at R35 per week. How much does that leave her for other expenses?
5. Peter needs 2000 bricks to build a garden wall. The cost is R275 per thousand bricks plus R40 delivery charge per thousand bricks. How much would he have to pay altogether?

Managing your money: Savings

Why save money?

People who plan their budgets and save money can have better lives. Saving money helps you get the things you want.

Medium-term savings are generally for those things you want in 1 to 5 years, like furniture, while long-term savings will pay for things you may need many years from now, like money for retirement.

INVESTIGATE ■□■□■□■□■□

Here are some places where you can save money:
1. Keep your money at home
2. Save your money in a group saving scheme or society
3. Put your money in an account at the bank or post office
4. Invest your money in insurance policies or unit trusts.

In groups investigate each of the above. Report back to the class on the topics under the headings advantages and disadvantages of each.

Simple interest

This is where you get interest on the money you invest only and not any interest on the interest you earn. So if you invest R100 at 10% simple interest per year (per annum is per year and written as p.a.) you will get R10 interest after 1 year. At the end of the second year you will get R10 again calculated on the original R100 and not on the R110 you now have.

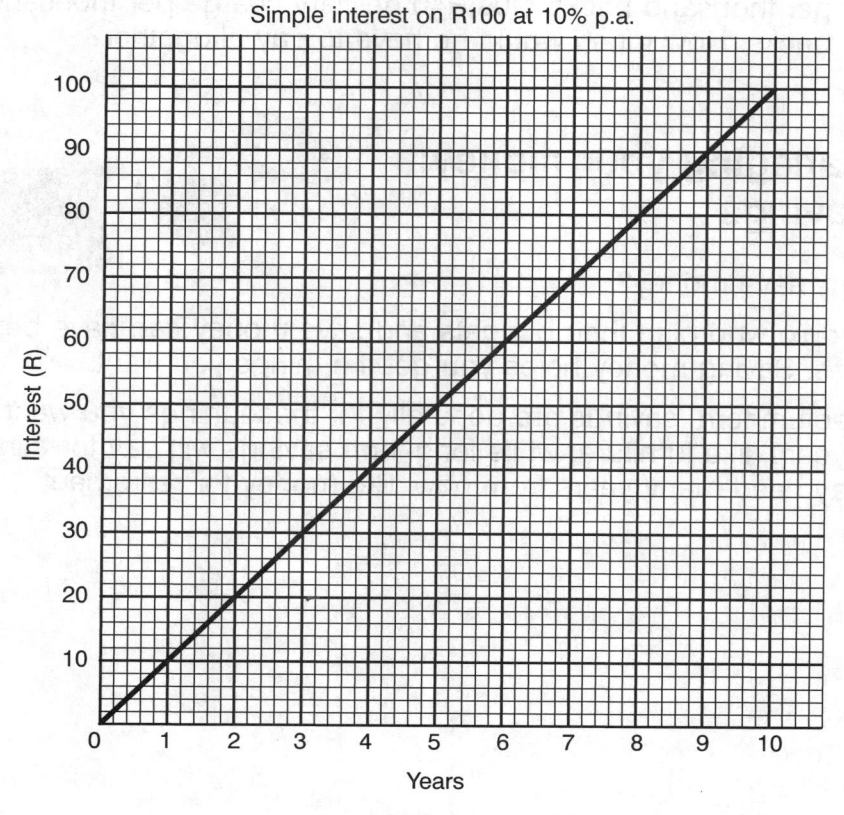

Simple interest on R100 at 10% p.a.

Exercise 5
1. From the graph, what is the interest for:
   a) 1 year   b) 2 years   c) 3 years   d) 10 years
2. What do you notice about the interest each year?
3. If you invested R200 at 10% you would get twice as much interest. What interest would you get on R200 for:
   a) 1 year   b) 2 years   c) 3 years   d) 10 years

We can calculate the simple interest using a formula:

Simple Interest = S.I. = $\frac{P \times r \times n}{100}$ = where: P is the amount of money invested
r is the rate of interest (% p.a.)
n is the number of years

So, R2000 is invested at 15% simple interest for 3 years. The amount of interest is:

P = 2000   S.I. = $\frac{P \times r \times n}{100}$
r = 15   = $\frac{2000 \times 15 \times 3}{100}$
n = 3   = 900

The money will earn R900 interest and the total money will now be R2900.

Exercise 6
1. Calculate the simple interest on R4000 at 13% for 2 years
2. Calculate the simple interest on R5 500 at 15% for 5 years
3. When she retired, Yolande invested her lump sum of R80 000 at 15% simple interest p.a. How much did it earn in the first year?
4. R1500 is invested at 12% p.a. What will the money be worth after 2 years?
5. An insurance company pays interest at a rate of 13% p.a. for amounts over R7000. How much is earned in 3 years on an investment of R9 500?

Exchange rates

Sometimes people need to travel overseas on business, or some people may take a holiday overseas.

Activity 3: Travel

Choose a country you want to travel to outside of South Africa. Discuss and find out about the preparations needed for travel overseas, such as passports, visas, travellers cheques, insurance, air tickets from travel agents and information on the country you would like to go to.

$ £ C ¥ IR

The exchange rates are used to calculated how much money you can buy in another country for the amount of money you have in your own currency. Travel agents, banks and the daily newspapers publish the rates of exchange, which vary from hour to hour.

Exchange Rates table

Country	What the bank will give you
USA	R6,25
UK	R10,20
Botswana	R1,40
Malawi	R0,1493
Zimbabwe	R0,1667

This means that 1 unit of USA currency gives R6,25 or 1 dollar is worth R6,25. Also, R1 is worth $\frac{1}{6,25} = \$0,16$

Exercise 7

Use the above table.
1. How much will 10 USA dollars cost?
2. You are travelling to Malawi. What will R2000 give you in Malawian currency?
3. What will R2000 give you in Zimbabwean dollars?
4. How much will 100 UK pounds cost?
5. How many UK pounds will R100 give you?

PROBLEM SOLVER

Sipho earns R5000 per month. Each year he gets an increase of 6%. He saves 10% of his salary every month. Lerato earns R5000 per month. Each year she gets an increase of 8%. She saves 8% of her salary every month. At the end of three years, who will have saved the most?

How did you do?

- Did you enjoy finding out about different types of professions?
- Did you understand how it works to be paid by commission?
- Could you calculate tax using the tax tables?
- Were you able to convert money to different currencies?
- Which section of this unit did you find the most interesting?
- Which section did you find the most difficult to understand?

UNIT 12

Planning a holiday

It is wonderful to be able to go on holiday but—it can cost quite a bit of money! Often a holiday is the result of many years of saving. That is why it is important to plan your holiday very carefully. This will allow you to make the most of the time that you have. Time is precious.

A holiday in another part of the country or in a foreign country gives us the chance to learn about other people; their customs, the food that they eat, their architecture (the style of their buildings) and their history. Learning about other people helps us to understand each other better.

Look at the picture above. Where do you think the family is going to? Where would you like to go on holiday? What are the sort of things that you would want to do on holiday?

In this unit you will

- be introduced to different time zones
- calculate time across geographical lines of longitude
- interpret data from graphs, charts and tables
- estimate and calculate distances on a map
- use formulae to calculate speed and time.

Activity 1: Planning a tour

You have been asked to be a tour guide for a day for your uncle's friends. They are visiting South Africa from England. They are very interested in learning about our ways of life, our traditions and culture. Draw up a plan of what you are going to do with them for the day. Include any places of interest or scenic views that they might enjoy. Include a list of people to whom you would like to introduce them. These could be family members or interesting people in the town. Suggest what food they should try and where to go. Think about how you will travel from place to place. Will you walk, go by car, or will you go by bus or taxi?

INVESTIGATE ■□■□■□■□

You are thinking about organising a football tour to either Cape Town, Durban or Bloemfontein during the June/July school holidays. One of the things to consider is the weather at that time of the year. The bar and line graphs below show the average yearly rainfall and temperature figures respectively for each month.

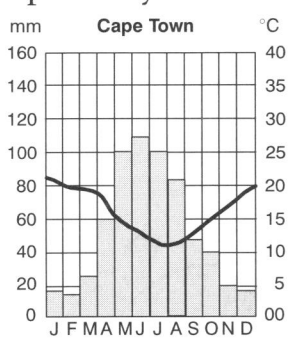

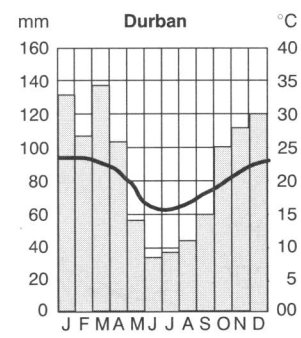

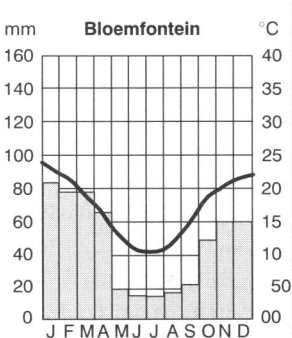

1. Which city has the most rain during June/July?
2. Which city has the least rain during June/July?
3. Which city is the coldest during June/July?
4. Which city has the warmest climate during June/July?
5. Which city would you choose for your football tour? Why?

Exercise 1: Going camping

The Zuma family and the Fortune family plan to go camping together at a nearby campsite. The Zuma family consists of 2 adults and 3 children aged 15, 8 and 18 months. The Fortune family consists of 2 adults and a child aged 10 years.

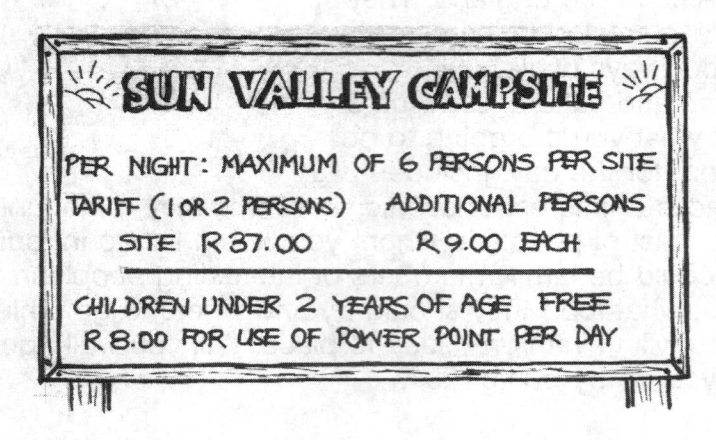

SUN VALLEY CAMPSITE

PER NIGHT: MAXIMUM OF 6 PERSONS PER SITE
TARIFF (1 OR 2 PERSONS)   ADDITIONAL PERSONS
SITE R 37.00   R 9.00 EACH

CHILDREN UNDER 2 YEARS OF AGE FREE
R 8.00 FOR USE OF POWER POINT PER DAY

1. How many sites will they need?
2. What will it cost per night for both families?
3. What will the total cost for 7 nights camping be?
4. They are asked to pay a 10% deposit when they book. How much do they have to pay?

Activity 2: Planning a holiday

The Peterson family are planning a holiday travelling around Zimbabwe. They are going to fly to Harare and then rent a car for their 10 day trip. They have planned the following route:

Harare to Nyanga
Nyanga to Mutare
Mutare to Chimanimani
Chimanimani to Masvingo
Masvingo to Bulawayo
Bulawayo to Victoria Falls
They will finally fly from Victoria Falls to Johannesburg.

						BULAWAYO
					CHIMANIMANI	560
				HARARE	404	445
			MASVINGO	292	279	281
		MUTARE	297	263	141	565
	NYANGA	107	404	311	248	613
VICTORIA FALLS	1046	998	714	878	989	433

	Make and Model	Daily & km rate	Long distance rates per day 300 kms free per day				Insurance per day		
			1-3 days	4-6 days	7-14 days	15 days +	with excess CDW	full dover CDW	TLW (reduced excess)
S	Super economy, no radio/tape, not available Johannesburg	59,0 69c per km	179,00	119,00	109,00	99,00	32,00	65,00	11,00
A	Opel Corsa 1,3 (3 door), VW Gold, Mazda Midge, Ford Tracer, Toyota Conquest	69,00 89c pe km	209,00	149,00	119,00	109,00	34,00	71,00	13,00
B	Opel kadett 1.6i, Ford Escort 1.6i, or similar man/air con	89,00 99c per km	269,00	199,00	149,00	139,00	37,00	76,00	14,00
C	Nissan Sentra 1.6 or similar auto/PAS/air con	119,00 129c per km	309,00	229,00	189,00	169,00	40,00	84,00	15,00
D	Ford Falcon 4,0 GLi, Ford Telstar 2,0 HLE, man/auto/PAS/air con	179,00 189c per km	419,00	329,00	239,00	229,0	49,00	94,00	18,00
E	Toyota Venture 1.8 10 seater, air con	139,00 149c per km	349,00	259,00	219,00	209,00	49,00	94,00	18,00
F	BMW 316i air con/PAS	225,00 225 c per km	499,00	369,00	279,00	259,00	49,00	97,00	21,00

Help the Petersons to plan and to work out the costs of their holiday. Work in pairs.

1. Calculate the total number of kilometres for their trip by car.
2. If they choose the long distance rates, how many free kilometres will they be given?
3. Work out the cost of renting a B Group car, first using the daily rate price and then comparing that to the long distance rates. Include full cover insurance.
4. Which would be the more economical (cheaper) rate to use?
5. The Petersons estimate that they will travel an additional 500 km during the trip. What is the total estimated distance? Are they still within the free km range?
6. They estimate that they will cover 9 km for every litre of petrol used. How many litres of petrol do they expect to use?
7. If the price of petrol in Zimbabwe is 5,40 Zimbabwean Dollars (ZD) per litre, how many Zimbabwean Dollars should they budget for petrol?
8. If the exchange rate is roughly R1,00 = ZD6,00, what is the petrol cost in Rands?

Estimating distances

It is often not necessary to know the exact distance between two places. An estimate to the nearest 10km or even 50km will do. We need to use a known distance and then compare the other distances to it. For example, the distance between Bulawayo and Plumtree is 100 km. One could then estimate that the distance between Bulawayo and Guyu is about 100 km as well.

Exercise 2

Use the map of Zimbabwe, and the known distance between Bulawayo and Plumtree, to estimate the following distances:
1. Bulawayo to Gweru
2. Harare to Mutare
3. Gweru to Harare.

The Petersons need to work out how long it will take them to drive from town to town in order to make the most of their time.

We use the formula TIME = DISTANCE/SPEED and decide that their average speed between towns will be 100 km per hour.

Example: How long will it take the Petersons to drive from Harare to Nyanga, travelling at 100 km per hour?
Solution, Time = Distance/Speed
           = 264 km/100
           = 2,64 hours

So it will take them just over two and a half hours.

Exercise 3

Travelling at 100 km per hour, how long will the following trips take?
1. Nyanga to Mutare.
2. Bulawayo to Victoria Falls.
3. Mutare to Chimanimani.

The trip from Mutare to Chimanimani is 151 km. However, it took them 2 hours.

4. At what speed were they travelling?
5. Why do you think they travelled slowly?
6. Calculate their speed if they took n hours to travel from Chimanimani to Masvingo. (Don't be put off by the n.)

Longitude

Lines of longitude are imaginary lines which run from north to south, from the one pole to the other. There is a difference of 1 hour between every 15 degrees of longitude. The earth rotates from west to east. When we travel in an easterly direction, we gain time, and when we travel westwards we lose time. International time is taken from the Greenwich Meridian, which is the name given to the 0 degrees line of longitude which passes through Greenwich in London.

South Africa's standard time is taken from the 30 degree line of longitude. This means that South Africa is 2 hours ahead of Greenwich time, or Greenwich Mean Time (GMT) as it is called. So if it is 15.00 GMT, it is already 17.00 in South Africa.

Exercise 4
1. If it is 09.00 GMT, what is the time in South Africa?
2. If it is 14.00 in South Africa, what is GMT?
   Here is a rough map of the world showing the Greenwich Meridian and the location of a few cities.

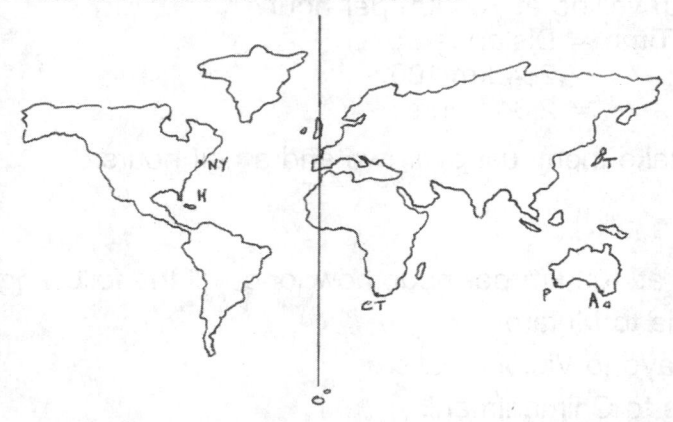

If GMT is 10.00, it will be 18.00 in Perth, Australia (approximately 120° E). What will the time be in
3. Adelaide (approx 135° E)
4. Tokyo (approx 135° E)
5. New York (approx 75° W)
6. If it is 13.00 in Durban, what is the time in Havana, Cuba? (approx 90° W)
7. What is the time difference between Perth and Havana?

Activity 3

Mr and Mrs Pillay have won a trip to London for a week as 1st Prize in a national competition. The prize includes bed and breakfast in a hotel and R4000 spending money.

In England, the currency used is the pound sterling. The exchange rate when the Pillays travelled was 1 Pound = R10,27.

1. How much spending money in pounds do the Pillays have?

   It is useful to estimate an exchange rate to work out the cost of items quickly. The Pillays use 1 Pound = R10,00 as a rough estimate.

2. Roughly how many pounds do the Pillays have, using the estimate?

3. The Pillays depart from Johannesburg Airport at 20.15. If the flight takes 11 hours, what is their arrival time in London, British time (GMT)?

4. They buy a 5-day rail card which enables them to travel around London on buses or trains. If it costs 48 pounds each, what would this be in rands?

5. If they travel after 10.00 am, they get a 20% discount. How much would they save?

6. Why do you think that people are encouraged to travel after 10.00?

7. The Pillays were walking past Big Ben when they noticed that the clock showed 13.20. What was the time in South Africa?

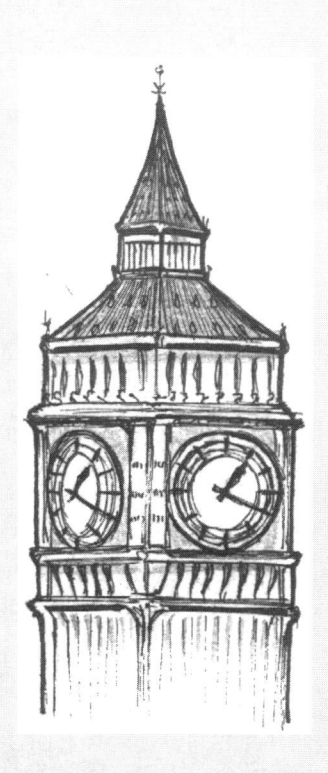

How did you do?

- Could you interpret the graphs showing rainfall and temperature?
- Were you able to read the distance chart and work out the distances between towns?
- Could you convert the different currencies?
- Were you able to estimate the distances reasonably and accurately?
- Could you use the formulae to calculate speed and time?
- Were you able to calculate time in the different countries?
- Which section did you find the hardest? Why was it so hard? What are you going to do about this section?

UNIT 13

What is the chance?

Look at the picture. Suppose you are the captain of the team and the umpire has asked you to call heads or tails. In your last match you called heads and lost the toss. What should you call now? Why? What is the chance of heads coming up this time? Can you think of other situations where you have to make a guess about the chances of something happening? Is there any pattern in the guesses that you make or do you just choose what you feel at the time? Is there a better way of making a choice so that you are correct more often?

In this unit you will be given the opportunity to:

- predict the chance of something happening
- test your prediction
- use a tree diagram to work out probability
- calculate probabilities using counting
- use a net diagram to make a die
- record data on a table
- read data from a table
- read probabilities from a graph.

Activity 1: Toss a coin

Work in groups of two. Toss a coin and record or count the number of times it comes up heads or tails. Draw your own table similar to the one shown below. Start by tossing the coin 10 times and record your results. Then toss the coin 30 times and record your results in the table. Continue until the table is completely filled. In the table below I have filled in the results of tossing a coin 10 times.

(In the column shown for ten tosses, I got 3 heads and 7 tails. So the fraction of heads is 3 out of 10, or $\frac{3}{10}$. Therefore the fraction of tails must be 7 out of 10 or $\frac{7}{10}$.

Example of table for results:

Number of tosses	10	10	30	50	100	200
Number of heads	3					
Number of tails	7					
Fraction of heads	$\frac{3}{10}$ = 0,3					
Fraction of tails	$\frac{7}{10}$ = 0,7					

1. Can you notice something about the fractions of heads or of tails as the number of tosses increases?

2. What would you say the chance of a coin landing with heads would be? Why?

3. Compare your results with other groups in the class. What fraction does the number of heads and tails seem to be getting closer and closer to?

Probability

When you toss a coin, the chance of landing heads is 50%, or 1 in 2 chances. We call this **probability** and we say the probability of getting heads is $\frac{1}{2}$.

The chance of rain

The map below shows the weather report for a particular day in September in South Africa. The marked areas show the percentage chance of rain falling in that area. The Weather Bureau has many weather stations around the country to record (write down) the rainfall patterns.

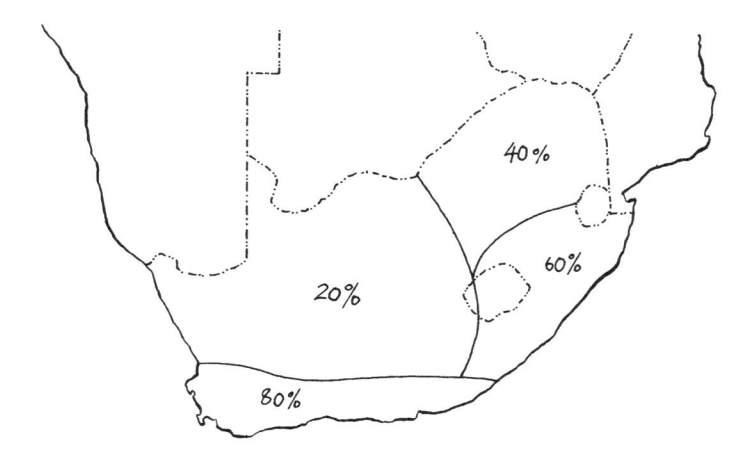

The area marked 40%, means, according to the Weather Bureau, they predict (expect) that 40% of the weather stations in that area will have rain. Since 40% = $\frac{40}{100}$ = $\frac{2}{5}$, this means that 2 out of every 5 stations in that area should get rain. If there were 10 stations in that area, it would mean that 4 of the stations should get rain. Why is this?

Exercise 1
1. What fraction of stations in the area marked 80% should get rain?
2. If there are 20 recording stations in the 80% area, how many of these should get rain?
3. In an area, if 3 out of 10 recording stations get rain, what is the percentage of rainfall in that area?
4. In an area, if 1 in 5 recording stations get rain, what is the percentage of rainfall in that area?
5. The day after the map was predicting rain, it was found that in the 40% area, 8 out of 30 recording stations actually got rain. Work out the percentage of rainfall in that area and compare it with the predicted value.

Tree diagrams

As we toss a coin we can record the various combinations by means of a tree diagram:

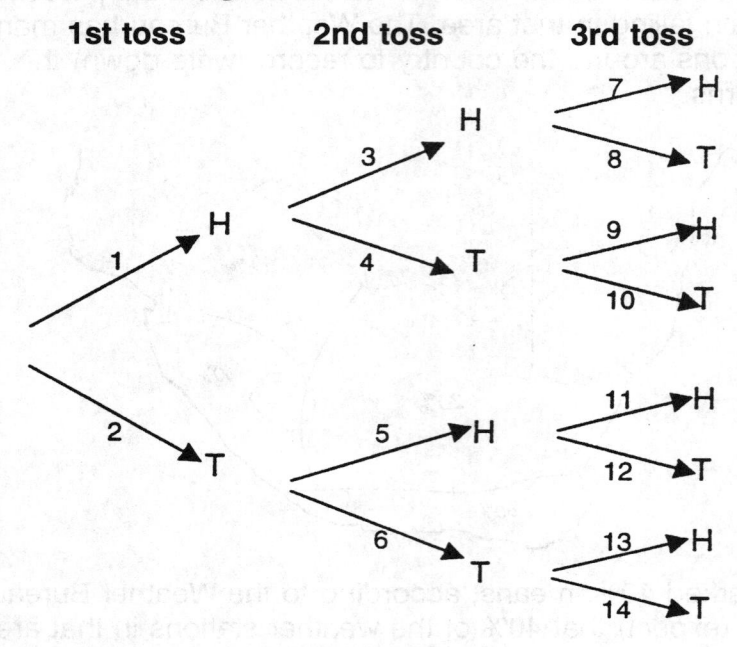

```
1st toss        2nd toss        3rd toss
                                    7 → H
                          H
                      3 →         8 → T
              H
          1 →             4 → T    9 → H
                                   10 → T

                                   11 → H
                      5 → H
          2 →                      12 → T
              T
                      6 → T        13 → H
                                   14 → T
```

H represents heads and T tails.

This diagram shows 3 tosses of a coin.

Arrows 1 and 2 represent the 1st toss. We can get heads or tails, which we show on arrow 1 with H and on arrow 2 with T. Because there are 2 possibilities when we toss a coin (H or T), we say that the possibility of getting H is 1 out of 2, (or $\frac{1}{2}$) and the possibility of getting T is also $\frac{1}{2}$.

Arrows 3, 4, 5 and 6 represent the 2nd toss. This means that if a coin is tossed twice, there are four possibilities: H then H (arrow 1 then 3); H then T (arrow 1 then 4); T then H (arrow 2 then 5); T then T (arrow 2 then 6).

In order to get both heads from the two tosses we want H then H. There is only one path we can follow to get this result so we say that the probability of getting 2 H from the 2 tosses is 1 out of the 4 possibilities.

We say the **probability** of getting two heads from two tosses of a coin is 1 in 4 or $\frac{1}{4}$.

Exercise 2

Use the tree diagram on page 126 to answer the following:
1. What is the probability of getting a head and a tail on two tosses of a coin?
2. What is the probability of getting a head and then a tail on two tosses of a coin?
3. How many possibilities are there if a coin is tossed three times?
4. What is the probability of getting three heads in a row on tossing a coin three times?

Boy or girl?

Women have 2 X chromosomes (XX) and men have 1 X and 1 Y chromosome (XY). When a baby is conceived, it gets 1 chromosome from each parent. Because the mother only has X chromosomes, she must give the baby an X chromosome. The father gives the baby either an X or a Y chromosome, so it is the father who determines the sex of the child.

In a family of two children, what is the possibility that both children are boys? This diagram can be used to see the number of possibilities.

1st child   2nd child

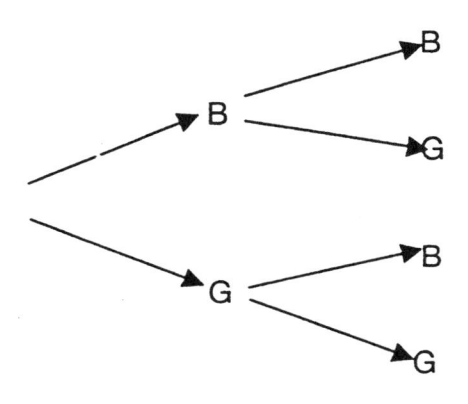

These are: Boy then boy
Boy then girl
Girl then boy
Girl then girl

This means that out of a total of four possibilities, we want one of them, so the **probability of both being boys is:** $\frac{1}{4}$.

Exercise 3
1. Draw up a tree diagram for a family of three children. Work out the probability of all three children being boys.
2. What is the probability that there are two boys and one girl?

Another way of working out the probabilities is using Pascal's triangle.

The triangle was named after Pascal, a 17th century pioneer in the field of probability.

Sum of numbers in a row

```
Sum : 2              1       1                  : first row
Sum : 4          1       2       1              : second row
Sum : 8      1       3       3       1          : third row
           1       4       6       4       1
```

The above represents Pascal's triangle for 4 rows.

The fourth row can represent a family of four children. If you add all the numbers in the fourth row you get 16. This represents the number of possibilities of 4 children. The 1 on either side represents the least possible outcome, that is 4 boys or four girls, which will have a probability of 1 in 16 or $\frac{1}{16}$. The four is made up of 1 and 3 and represents the probability of having 1 girl and 3 boys (or 1 boy and 3 girls) which is 4 in 16 or $\frac{4}{16} = \frac{1}{4}$. The 6 is made up of 3 and 3 and represents the same number of boys and girls i.e. 2 boys and 2 girls with a probability of 6 in 16 or $\frac{6}{16} = \frac{3}{8}$.

Exercise 4
1. See if you can follow the pattern and complete the 5th row.

Now use the 5th row to answer the following:
2. What is the probability of having 5 boys in a family of 5 children?
3. What is the probability of having 4 girls and 1 boy?

INVESTIGATE ■□■□■□■□

Look at all the four children families in your school. Work out the probabilities of all the different combinations of boys and girls. Compare your results with the probabilities suggested by Pascal's triangle and try to give reasons for any differences.

Kaizer Chiefs to win?

We are going to make use of tree diagrams for soccer teams playing in a knock-out tournament.

Suppose the chance of each team winning is the same. Therefore we say the probability of a team winning each match (or losing) is $\frac{1}{2}$.

We can design a tree diagram as follows:

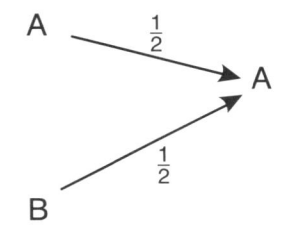

A $\xrightarrow{\frac{1}{2}}$ A

B $\xrightarrow{\frac{1}{2}}$

This means that teams A and B play each other and team A wins. The fractions show that the probability of A (or B) winning is $\frac{1}{2}$.

Let us look at the knock-out competition between 8 teams:

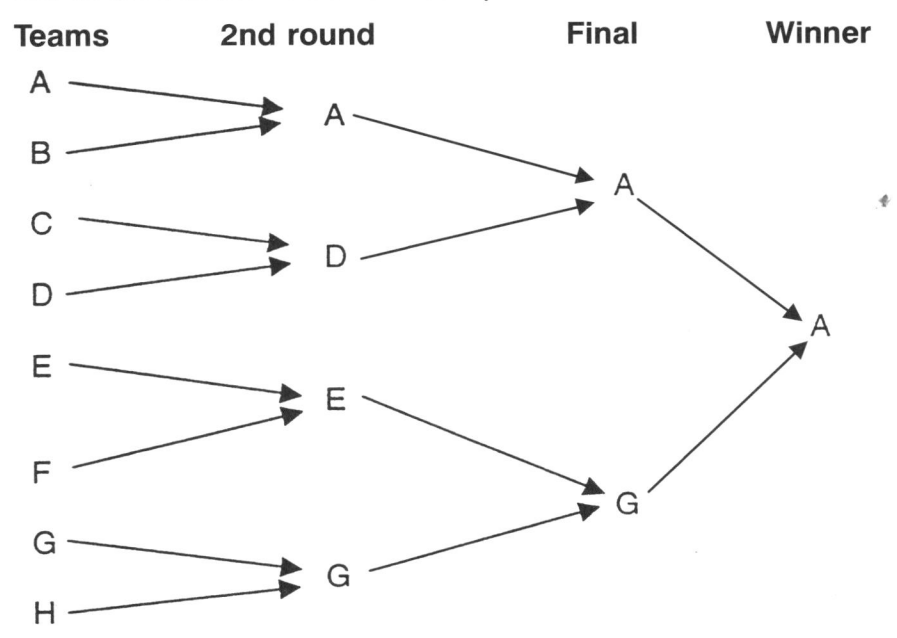

Teams	2nd round	Final	Winner
A	A		
B		A	
C	D		
D			A
E	E		
F		G	
G	G		
H			

Exercise 5

1. If each line represents a probability of $\frac{1}{2}$, what is the probability of A making the 2nd round?
2. What is the probability of G making the finals?

For G to make the finals, they have to beat H **and** E. This is harder than just beating H, so the probability should be less.

To beat H is $\frac{1}{2}$ **AND** to beat E is $\frac{1}{2}$. So the probability of beating both sides is $\frac{1}{2} \times \frac{1}{2} = \frac{1}{4}$

3. Work out the probability that A won the tournament.

Throwing dice

Activity 2: Make your own dice

Work in groups of 4.

You are going to make your own dice using cardboard. Copy the net diagram shown below onto some cardboard. Fold along the dotted lines and glue the flaps down. The numbers must be on the outside, and the numbers on opposite sides of the dice must add up to 7.

Make two of these dice. (The singular is die, the plural is dice, therefore we say one die and two dice.)

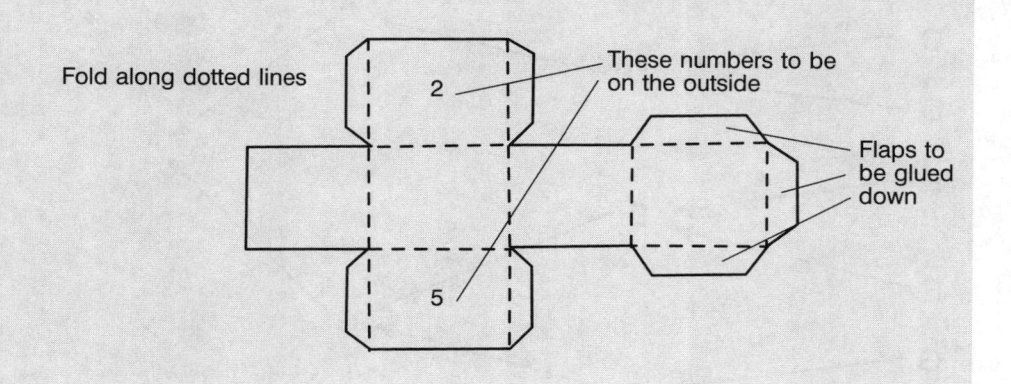

You can use different coloured paper for the two dice if you want to. Throw both dice together and record the sum of the faces showing on top, so for example the sum of the following dice is
3 + 4 = 7.

Activity 3: Rolling dice.

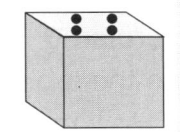

1. Write down all the possible combinations when two dice are rolled. (Remember, 1 on the first die and 2 on the second die is different from 2 on the first die and 1 on the second die.)
2. What are the possible totals that can come up?

Draw a tally table like the one shown and after each throw record your result with a one. So:

Total on dice	2	3	4	5	6	7	8	9	10	11	12
Number of times it comes up	11	1		1	111						

In my table a total of 2 has come up twice, a total of 3 once, a total of 5 once and a total of 6 three times. Now do your own table, but make it big enough to include all the possibilities of totals that can come up. Then toss the dice **100 times**.

3. What is the total that comes up most often? Why?
4. What is the total(s) that come up least often? Why?

Compare your results with other groups.

5. Do you think there is a better way to record your data?

Possible totals on two dice

		\multicolumn{6}{c}{The number showing on one die}
		1	2	3	4	5	6
The number showing on the other die	1	2	3	4	5	6	7
	2	3	4	5	6	7	8
	3	4	5	6	7	8	9
	4	5	6	7	8	9	10
	5	6	7	8	9	10	11
	6	7	8	9	10	11	12

On the top are the numbers showing on one die and on the left are the number showing on the other die. **The table itself shows the totals that the two dice can add up to.**

Exercise 6

Use the table to answer the following questions:
1. How many combinations of totals are there?
2. What is the most common total?
3. Write the fraction and simplify:

   $$\frac{\text{the number of times the most common total occurs}}{\text{the number of possible totals}}$$
4. Write the fraction and simplify:

   $$\frac{\text{the number of times the least common total occurs}}{\text{the number of possible totals}}$$

Possible or impossible?

The probability of something that cannot occur (that is the event is **impossible**) we give a probability of 0.
The probability of something that will definitely occur (that is the event is **a certainty**) we give a probability of 1.
Everything else will have a fractional value between 0 and 1. (It will be a fraction.)

Activity 4:

Discuss in groups of 2:

1. Give examples of events that have a probability of 0
2. Give examples of events that have a probability of 1
3. Give examples of events that have a probability of $\frac{1}{2}$
4. Give an example of an event that will have a probability of $\frac{3}{4}$

PROBLEM SOLVER

In Pascal's Triangle, the sum of each row can be calculated. Can you see a pattern in the sum of each row? What will the sum for the 20th row be? Can you derive a formula to find the sum for any row?

Reading from a graph

The following graph shows the probability of two or more people sharing a birthday out of a group of people:

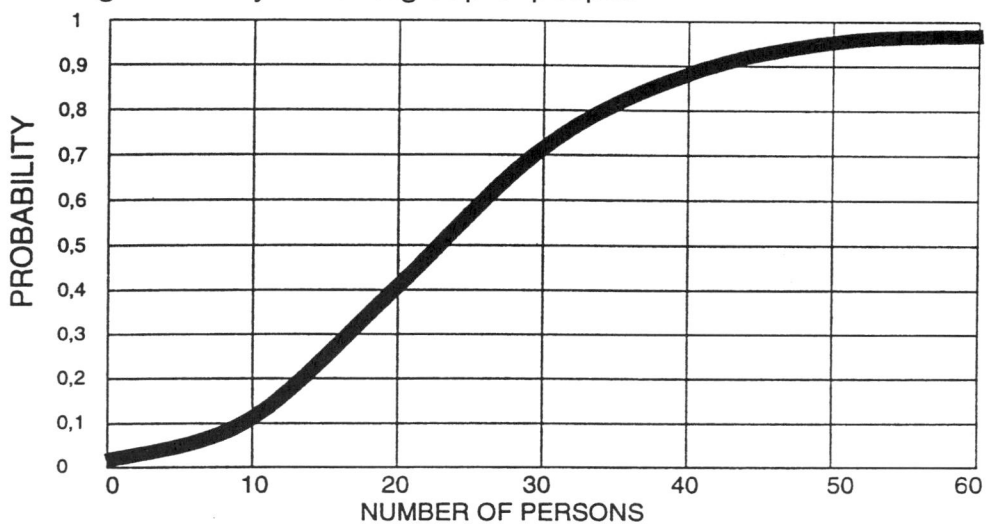

Exercise 7

1. If there is a group of 10 people, what is the probability of 2 people sharing a birthday?
2. If there is a group of 40 people, what is the probability of two people sharing a birthday?
3. Take the number of people in your class. Use the table to determine the probability of two people sharing a birthday. Then check in your class to see if anyone does in fact share a birthday.
4. If the probability of two people sharing a birthday is 0,7 what group size is needed?

How did you do?

- How did your results for the tossing of the coin compare with others in the class? If your results were totally different than expected, can you think of a reason why.
- Did you understand how to read a tree diagram?
- Could you use Pascal's triangle to work out probabilities of girls and boys?
- Which section did you find the most interesting?
- Is there any section of this unit that still bothers you?

UNIT 14

Numeracy skills

14.1 Fractions

Equivalent Fractions

Example

Change $\frac{3}{5}$ to tenths

$\frac{3}{5} = \frac{6}{10}$

(Multiply top and bottom by 2.)

Exercise 1

1. $\frac{1}{2} = \frac{?}{10}$ 2. $\frac{2}{3} = \frac{?}{9}$
3. $\frac{3}{4} = \frac{?}{12}$ 4. $\frac{4}{5} = \frac{8}{?}$
5. $\frac{7}{11} = \frac{21}{?}$ 6. $\frac{5}{8} = \frac{?}{24}$

Reducing to lowest terms

Example

Reduce $\frac{4}{16}$ to lowest terms

$\frac{4}{16} = \frac{1}{4}$

(Divide top and bottom by 4.)

Exercise 2

1. $\frac{5}{15}$ 2. $\frac{12}{20}$
3. $\frac{12}{24}$ 4. $\frac{8}{36}$
5. $\frac{16}{18}$ 6. $\frac{12}{40}$

Changing to mixed fractions

Example

Change $\frac{7}{2}$ to a mixed fraction.

$\frac{7}{2} = 3\frac{1}{2}$

(2 into 7 goes 3, remainder 1.

Exercise 3

1. $\frac{9}{4}$ 2. $\frac{11}{3}$
3. $\frac{13}{5}$ 4. $\frac{12}{7}$
5. $\frac{41}{8}$ 6. $\frac{37}{6}$

Changing to top-heavy fractions

Example

Change $2\frac{1}{5}$ into a top-heavy fraction.

($2 = \frac{10}{5}$, add $\frac{1}{5}$; equals $\frac{11}{5}$)

Exercise 4

1. $3\frac{1}{3}$ 2. $1\frac{3}{4}$
3. $1\frac{3}{5}$ 4. $2\frac{4}{7}$
5. $4\frac{5}{6}$ 6. $1\frac{7}{9}$

Addition

Example

Add $2\frac{1}{2}$ to $3\frac{2}{3}$

Add the whole numbers 2 and 3 to get 5.

Change $\frac{1}{2}$ and $\frac{2}{3}$ to equivalent fractions with the same denominator and add:

$$2\frac{1}{2} + 3\frac{2}{3} = 5 + \frac{3}{6} + \frac{4}{6}$$
$$= 5 + \frac{7}{6}$$
$$= 6\frac{1}{6}$$

Exercise 5

1. $\frac{1}{3} + \frac{1}{2}$
2. $\frac{2}{3} + \frac{1}{4}$
3. $1\frac{3}{5} + \frac{1}{10}$
4. $2\frac{2}{3} + 1\frac{3}{4}$
5. $2\frac{3}{5} + 1\frac{2}{3}$
6. $2\frac{5}{12} + 1\frac{1}{4}$

Subtraction

Example

From $1\frac{3}{5}$ subtract $\frac{2}{3}$

$$1 + \frac{9}{15} - \frac{10}{15} = \frac{15}{15} + \frac{9}{15} - \frac{10}{15}$$
$$= \frac{14}{15}$$

Exercise 6

1. $2\frac{3}{4} - 1\frac{1}{2}$
2. $1\frac{5}{6} - \frac{2}{3}$
3. $1\frac{1}{4} - \frac{2}{5}$
4. $3\frac{1}{3} - \frac{3}{4}$
5. $2\frac{1}{8} - 1\frac{1}{2}$
6. $3\frac{1}{5} - 2\frac{2}{3}$

Multiplication

Example

Multiply: $1\frac{2}{3} \times 2\frac{4}{5}$

Make fractions top-heavy:

$\frac{5}{3} \times \frac{14}{5} = \frac{14}{3}$ (cancelling 5's)

$\phantom{\frac{5}{3} \times \frac{14}{5}} = 4\frac{2}{3}$ (changing to mixed fractions)

Exercise 7

1. $\frac{1}{3} \times \frac{4}{5}$
2. $\frac{2}{3} \times \frac{9}{16}$
3. $2\frac{2}{5} \times \frac{5}{8}$
4. $2\frac{2}{3} \times 1\frac{1}{4}$
5. $2\frac{1}{2} \times \frac{1}{7} \times 1\frac{1}{5}$
6. $(2\frac{1}{4})^2$

Division

Example

Divide $1\frac{1}{2}$ by $\frac{3}{4}$

Make fractions top-heavy:

$\frac{3}{2} \div \frac{3}{4}$

Turn the second fraction upside down and multiply.

$\frac{3}{2} \times \frac{4}{3} = 2$

Exercise 8

1. $\frac{3}{5} \div \frac{27}{10}$
2. $\frac{1}{2} \div \frac{1}{12}$
3. $1\frac{5}{8} \div \frac{1}{2}$
4. $2\frac{1}{4} \div 1\frac{1}{2}$
5. $3\frac{1}{4} \div 1\frac{5}{8}$
6. $3\frac{1}{2} \div 7$

Changing fractions to decimals

$\frac{1}{2}$ means $1 \div 2$. Writing 1 as 1,0 we get

$$\begin{array}{r} 0{,}5 \\ 2\overline{)1{,}0} \end{array}$$

Exercise 9

Change to decimals, correcting to 3 decimal places if necessary:

1. $\frac{2}{5}$
2. $\frac{1}{4}$
3. $\frac{1}{3}$
4. $\frac{2}{3}$
5. $\frac{1}{8}$
6. $1\frac{4}{7}$

Changing decimals to fractions

Example

$0{,}2 = \frac{2}{10} = \frac{1}{5}$

$1{,}31 = 1 + \frac{3}{10} + \frac{1}{100} = 1\frac{31}{100}$

Exercise 10

Change to fractions:

1. 0,7   2. 0,6   3. 1,25
4. 0,375   5. 4,6   6. 5,21

Changing percentages to fractions

Percent means *out of 100*.

$4\% = \frac{4}{100} = \frac{1}{25}$

Exercise 11

Change these percentages to fractions in lowest terms:

1. 10%   2. 20%
3. 25%   4. 7%
5. 120%   6. $12\frac{1}{2}\%$

Changing fractions to percentages

To change a fraction to a percentage multiply by 100%.

Example

$\frac{1}{3} = \frac{1}{3} \times 100\% = \frac{100}{3}\% = 33\frac{1}{3}\%$

Exercise 12

Change these fractions to percentages:

1. $\frac{2}{5}$ 2. $\frac{1}{4}$

3. $\frac{1}{3}$ 4. $\frac{3}{8}$
5. $\frac{11}{20}$ 6. $1\frac{1}{2}$

Mixed examples

1. What is the total mass of seven $2\frac{1}{2}$ kg bags of sugar?
2. Divide a piece of piping $13\frac{1}{2}$ metres long into 4 equal pieces.
3. Seven $1\frac{1}{2}$ litre cans are filled from a container holding $35\frac{1}{2}$ litres of petrol. How much petrol is left in the container?
4. Nana takes half an hour to walk to the bus stop. She spends $1\frac{1}{4}$ hours on the bus, then stands for $2\frac{3}{4}$ hours in a queue to buy tickets for a concert. It takes her 2 hours to return home. How long is she away from home?
5. In a class, $\frac{1}{4}$ of the learners are less than 12 years old and $\frac{2}{5}$ are more than 14 years old. What fraction of the class are 12, 13 or 14 years old?
6. 23 in a group of 40 are boys. What percentage is that?

Self assessment

1. Fill in the missing numbers:
   (a) $\frac{1}{3} = \frac{?}{9}$ (b) $\frac{3}{8} = \frac{?}{64}$
2. Reduce to lowest terms:
   (a) $\frac{6}{8}$ (b) $\frac{6}{20}$
3. Change to mixed fractions:
   (a) $\frac{19}{2}$ (b) $\frac{35}{16}$

4. Change to top-heavy fractions:
   (a) $2\frac{1}{4}$ (b) $3\frac{2}{3}$
5. Work out:
   (a) $2\frac{1}{2} + 1\frac{3}{8}$ (b) $1\frac{1}{4} - \frac{1}{2}$
   (c) $2\frac{2}{5} \times 1\frac{2}{3}$ (d) $6\frac{1}{2} \div \frac{3}{4}$
6. Write $1\frac{3}{4}$ as a decimal.
7. Write 0,7 and 3% as fractions.
8. Write 30% as a fraction.

14.2 Money Calculations, (percentage, interest, profit and loss)

Percentage

Four per cent means 4 out of every 100. A 4% wage increase means that for every R100 you earn you will get an extra R4. If you earned R800 you would get R4 x 8 more. If you earned R3 000, you would get R4 x 30 = R120 more.

Exercise 1

How much extra would you earn if you had:
1. a 3% increase on R500?
2. 10% on R700?
3. 5% on R900?
4. 8% on R1 000?
5. 9% on R2 000?
6. 2% on R1 500?
7. 1% on R9 500?
8. 7% on R1 200?
9. 4.5% on R8 000?
10. 2,5% on R6 000?

It is easy to find, say, 30% of R600 using a calculator. Without a calculator, you would first find 1% of R600, which is R6, so 30% would be 30 x R6 which is R180. To work out 1%, you move the decimal point 2 places to the left. To work out 10%, move the decimal point 1 place to the left.

Example

1% of R350 = R3,50 (divide by 100)

10% of R12,50 = R1,25 (divide by 10)

It is useful to know the common fractions and their decimal equivalents.

Percent	Fraction	Decimal
1% =	$\frac{1}{100}$ =	0,01
5% =	$\frac{1}{20}$ =	0,05
10% =	$\frac{1}{10}$ =	0,10
12,5% =	$\frac{1}{8}$ =	0,125
15% =	$\frac{3}{20}$ =	0,15
25% =	$\frac{1}{4}$ =	0,25
30% =	$\frac{3}{10}$ =	0,30
$33\frac{1}{3}$% =	$\frac{1}{3}$ =	$0,\dot{3}$
50% =	$\frac{1}{2}$ =	0,50
75% =	$\frac{3}{4}$ =	0,75

Exercise 2
1. 10% of R530
2. 5% of R700
3. 1% of R9
4. 12,5% of R16
5. 25% of R5
6. 75% of R12
7. 10% of R55
8. $33\frac{1}{3}$% of R660
9. 17% of R504
10. 5% of R6 897
11. In a sale, all items are reduced by 4%. How much do we pay if the goods are marked at R200?
12. A 20% discount is given on a R250 coat. How much do we pay?
13. A R132 dress is increased by 25%. What is the increase?
14. A surcharge of 10% is made on a R1 500 air ticket. What must we now pay?

Simple interest

When you save your money with a bank then extra money, called interest, is paid to you while you save.

Examples
1. You save R525 for 2 years at a rate of 12% simple interest per year. How much interest do you earn?

For one year the interest would be R525 ÷ 100 x 12 = R63. Therefore for 2 years the interest is 2 x R63 = R126.

Note that with simple interest, if the time or period is 2 years, then the interest is doubled, for three years it is tripled, for 6 months it is halved etc.

You could use the simple interest formula

$$I = \frac{P \times R \times T}{100}$$

where P is the principal or amount of the loan, R is the rate of interest as a percentage, T is the time of the loan in years, and I is the interest.

2. Find the simple interest on R6 470 loaned for 3 years at 8% interest.

P = 6470, R = 8, T = 3 so, using the formula

$$I = \frac{6470 \times 8 \times 3}{100}$$
$$= R1552,80$$

Exercise 3

Find the simple interest on:
1. R7250 at 8% for 2 years
2. R4100 at 11% for 3 years
3. R4800 at 12% for 7 years
4. R1840 at 9% for 6 months
5. R200 at 7% for 1 year and 6 months
6. R282,50 at 15% for 10 years

Compound interest

If the interest is added to your loan or your savings at the end of each year, then the interest also earns interest. This is called compound interest.

Examples

Method 1

Find the compound interest earned on R1700 invested at 10% for 2 years.

Interest at end of 1st year
= 10% of R1700 = R170.

Total amount at the end of 1st year = R1700 + R170 = R1870.

Interest at the end of 2nd year
= 10% of R1870 = R187.

Total amount at end of 2nd year
= R1870 + R187 = R2057.

Compound interest is
R2057 - R1700 = R357.

Note that the interest in the second year is more than the interest in the first year

Method 2

Find (a) the final amount and (b) the compound interest on R700 at 9% invested for 4 years.

To find the amount at the end of one year at 9% of R700. You could do this by multiplying R700 by $\frac{109}{100}$.

To find the amount (savings plus interest) at the end of the second year, again multiply by $\frac{109}{100}$.

The final amount after 4 years is

R700 × $\frac{109}{100}$ × $\frac{109}{100}$ × $\frac{109}{100}$ × $\frac{109}{100}$

= R700 × 1,09 × 1,09 × 1,09 × 1,09

= R988,11 (to the nearest cent.)

Exercise 4

Find (a) the final amount and (b) the compound interest on

1. R3000 invested for 2 years at 10%.
2. R600 invested for 2 years at 10%.
3. R7050 invested for 3 years at 4%.
4. R4500 invested for 3 years at 4%.
5. R1800 invested for 2 years at 9%.
6. R6750 invested for 4 years at 6%.

Writing a number as a percentage of another number

To express a number as a percentage of another number, just write as a fraction and then convert to a percentage by multiplying by 100%.

Example

What is R35 as a percentage of R40?

$\frac{35}{40} = \frac{35}{40} \times 100\%$

$= \frac{175}{2}$

$= 87,5\%$

Exercise 5

Write the first number as a percentage of the second.

1. R5, R20
2. R250, R500
3. R3, R60
4. R8, R40

5. R5, R50   6. R2, R800
7. 75c, R2,40   8. R2,50, R1,00

Profit and loss

If goods are bought for R50 and sold for R55, then a profit of R5 has been made. The R50 is known as the cost price and the R55 as the selling price.

Profit = selling price − cost price

Percentage profit

$= \dfrac{SP - CP}{CP} \times 100\%$

So, % profit $= \dfrac{R55 - R50}{R50} \times 100\%$

$= \dfrac{5}{50} \times 100\%$

$= 10\%$

Exercise 6

Copy the table and fill in the missing figures.

Cost price	Selling price	Profit	% Profit
R100	R104	.....	.....
R500	R550	.....	.....
R250	R260	.....	.....
R8,00	R16	.....	.....
R0,45	R0,50	.....	.....

When the selling price is less than the cost price, then a loss has been made.

loss = cost price − selling price

Percentage loss

$= \dfrac{CP - SP}{CP} \times 100\%$

Example

A car is bought for R6500 and sold for R4000. What is (a) the loss, (b) the percentage loss?

(a) loss = CP − SP
 = R6500 − R4000
 = R2500

(b) percentage loss

$= \dfrac{R6500 - R4000}{R6500} \times 100\%$

$= \dfrac{R2500}{R6500} \times 100\%$

$= 38{,}5\%.$

Exercise 7

Copy the table and fill in the missing figures

Cost price	Selling price	Loss	% loss
R100	R97	.....	.....
R250	R200	.....	.....
R0,50	R0,40	.....	.....
R18	R12,50	.....	.....
R60	R50	.....	.....

Suppose you know the percentage profit (or loss) and the cost price, but have to find the selling price.

Example

A suite of furniture is sold at a 5% loss. It was bought for R500. What is the selling price?

The loss is 5% of the cost price

$= \dfrac{5}{100} \times R500$

$= R25$

The suite was sold for R500 − R25 = R475.

Exercise 8

Copy the table and fill in the missing figures.

Cost price	Selling price	Profit or loss	% Profit or loss
R700	.....	...loss	5% loss
R400	.....	...loss	10% loss
R350	.....	...profit	2% profit
R600	.....	...profit	15% profit
R2250	.....	...loss	9% loss

You need to use a different method if you know the selling price and the percentage profit (or loss), and need to know the cost price.

Example

1. Profit

A coat was sold for R520 at 4% profit. How much did it cost?
104% = R520
  1% = R520 ÷ 104
So 100% = R520 ÷ 104 × 100
       = R500
The coat was bought for R500.

2. Loss

Find the cost of a suit sold for R188 at a loss of 6%
The cost price is 100% and the loss is 6%, so the selling price is equivalent to 94%.
94% = R188
 1% = R188 ÷ 94
So 100% = R188 ÷ 94 × 100
       = R200
The suit cost R200.

Exercise 9

This exercise is more difficult than the ones before. Copy the table and fill in the missing figures.

Cost price	Selling price	Profit or loss	Percentage profit/loss
.....	R115	...profit	15% profit
.....	R78	...profit	4% profit
.....	R36,75	...profit	5% profit
.....	R470	...loss	6% loss
.....	R1,96	...loss	2% loss
.....	R24	...loss	4% loss

Exercise 10

1. A video is sold for R550 and it cost the shop R500 to buy. Give the percentage profit.
2. If a table and chairs have a cost price of R200 and a selling price of R175, give the loss as a percentage of the cost price.
3. How much profit has been made if a television which cost R250 is sold for R270? Express this as a percentage.
4. A 5% profit is made when selling a desk which cost R120. What is the selling price?
5. Find the price at which a set of cassettes was sold if there was a 3% loss on the cost price of R25.
6. The selling price of a kettle is R62,60. It is sold at 5% profit. What is the cost price?

Exercise 11

1. If the rate of inflation is 16%, by how much would the price of goods costing R500 have risen a) the following year, b) after 2 years?
2. Gill borrows R1400 for 2 years. Calculate a) the simple interest at 16% per year payable on this loan b) the monthly repayments if the loan plus interest is paid back over 2 years.
3. A car depreciates by 12% of its value at the beginning of the year each year for 3 years. If it is valued at R5120 at the beginning of 1990, what is its value at the beginning of 1993?
4. R1 000 is invested at 10% per annum compound interest. How much will it amount to after a) 1 year b) 2 years? c)What investment would amount to R6050 after 2 years at compound interest?
5. A man's income is cut first by 5% and then by a further 2%. If he was originally on a salary of R10 000, calculate his final salary. Explain why this is not the same as a 7% salary cut.

End Test

1. Find
   (a) 1% of R72
   (b) 20% of R350
   (c) 12,5% of 72
   (d) 15% of R4500
2. Find (a) the simple interest at 7% on R806 for i) 2 years ii) 6 months
   (b) the compound interest at 5% on R7500 for 3 years.
3. Write
   (a) R45 as a percentage of R400
   (b) R9 as a percentage of R36.
4. A TV costs the retailer R1600 and is sold for R1750. Find the percentage profit.
5. What is the selling price if a video is bought by a shop for R385 and sold at 8% profit?
6. A suite of furniture is sold at 10% profit for R495. What was the cost price? Find the cost price of a TV sold at R364 for a 4% profit.
7. Wages fall from R4000 to R3500. What percentage drop is this?

14.3 Directed numbers

Directed numbers are positive and negative numbers, for example 5, -1, -2, +0,3 and so on.

Positive numbers have a value greater than zero. Negative numbers have a value less than zero. If there is no sign the number is assumed to be positive. You will have seen negative numbers on graphs.

Example

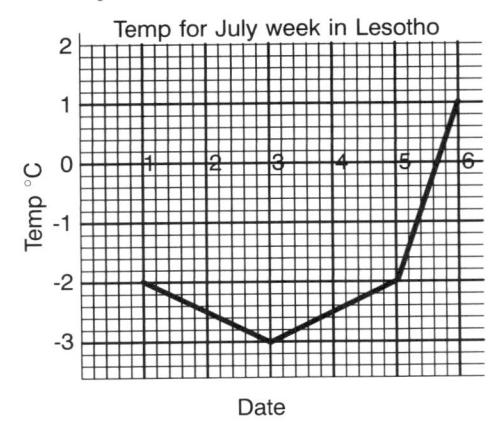

Temp for July week in Lesotho

(graph showing temperature from 2°C down to -3°C and back up to 1°C across dates 1-6)

The graph shows that the temperature rose by 4°C between 3rd and 6th of July. The difference between 1°C and -3° is 4°C.

Exercise 1

1. A liquid is cooled from 7°C to -5°C in 4 minutes.

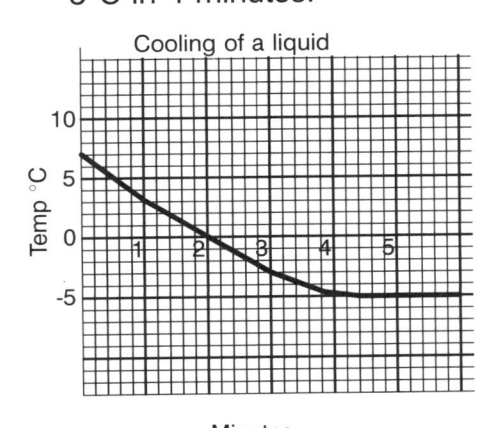

   Cooling of a liquid

   (graph showing temperature dropping from 10°C to -5°C over 5 minutes)

   (a) By how many degrees has its temperature dropped?
   (b) How long did it take to cool from 0°C to -5°C?
   (c) What will be its temperature if it cools a further 3°C after reaching -5°C?

2. A metal plate at a temperature of 4°C is cooled by 14°C. What is its temperature now?

3. Thandi arrived 6 minutes early for her train which was 10 minutes late. How long did she have to wait? Her friend, Sipho, arrived 3 minutes after the time at which the train should have departed. How long did Sipho have to wait?

4. The alarm clock is 7 minutes slow and the wall clock is 6 minutes fast. Give the difference in times shown by the two clocks.

5. BC means before Christ was born and AD means after Christ was born.

   (a) How old was a man born in 20 BC who dies in 20 AD?
   (b) In which year would a woman who died in 4 BC at an age of 36 have been born?

6. The number of hours ahead of or behind Greenich Mean Time (GMT) for five cities is given below:

City	Hours ahead of or behind GMT
New York	-3
Moscow	+2
San Francisco	-8
Sydney	+10
Mexico City	-7

(a) At 8 a.m. GMT what is the time in (1) New York (2) Sydney?

(b) If it is 2 p.m. in Moscow what is the time in Mexico City?

(c) How many hours ahead of San Francisco is (1) Mexico City (2) Moscow?

(d) How many hours behind Sydney is (1) New York (2) San Francisco?

(e) On 5th March at 3 p.m. in San Francisco what is the time and date in Sydney?

7. (a) Thabo owes the bank R186. He repays R150. How much does he owe now? He pays in a further cheque for R97. By how much will he now be in credit (credit means he has money in the bank and debit means he owes the bank money, usually referred to as an overdraft).

(b) Copy the bank statement shown below and fill in the right-hand column. Show overdrawn amounts by writing the letters OD after the amount.

BANK STATEMENT			
Date	Payments	Receipts	Balance
3 Sep			326,25
6 Sep	328,50		2,25 OD
7 Sep		342,25	342,25
12 Sep	140,55		
20 Sep	60,00		
28 Sep	180,00		
3 Oct		248,80	

8. The table below shows the height above or below sea level for various places in the world.

Place	Height above or below sea level
Mount Everest	+ 8848 m
The Dead Sea	- 395 m
Kilimanjaro	+ 5 895 m
Mariana Trench	- 11 022 m

Find the difference in height between:

(a) Kilimanjaro and Mount Everest

(b) Mount Everest and the Dead Sea

(c) Mount Everest and the Mariana Trench

9. The table below shows the temperature in the first week in July in Lesotho:

Temperature	Day
-6°C	1st July
-9°C	2nd July
-2°C	3rd July
-1°C	4th July
3°C	5th July
5°C	6th July
7°C	7th July

What is the difference in temperature between:

(a) the coldest and the warmest day?
(b) 2nd July and 3rd July?

10.

(a) Steps on a staircase have numbers painted on them as shown above. If Jo plays a game that starts on step 0, going up 1 step and back down 3 steps, then up 1 step and back down 3 steps, on which step will Jo now be standing?
(b) Taking +2 to mean up 2 steps, and -7 to mean down 7 steps, and so on, which step will Jo be on if she goes +2 − 7 + 3 steps starting from 0?
(c) Supposing Jo starts on step 0, goes down 2 steps and then down a further 2 steps, which number step will she be standing on?

11. My watch is 6 minutes slow.
(a) If I arrive at the bus stop at 10.34 a.m. by my watch, what is the actual time?
(b) The bus is supposed to leave at 10.40 a.m. but in fact leaves 8 minutes late. How long was I waiting for the bus?
(c) The journey is supposed to take 30 minutes but in fact takes 25 minutes. Does it arrive at its destination late or early and by how much?
(d) What time does my watch show when I arrive?

Using a calculator with directed numbers:

To make a number negative on a calculator press the +/- key directly after entering the number. To enter -5 press keys

| 5 | +/- |

Example

1. Calculate 5 + (-2)

Press keys | 5 | + | 2 | +/- | = |

Resulting in 3 on the display.

Calculate -19 + 13 -(-17)

Press keys

| 1 | 9 | +/- | + | 1 | 3 | - | 1 | 7 | +/- | = |

to get 11.

3. Work out - 7 x - 12

Press the keys

| 7 | +/- | x | 1 | 2 | +/- | = |

to get 84.

Order of Operations

Brackets must be done first, then x and ÷ and finally + and −. Otherwise work from left to right. A number outside the bracket means multiply. Sometimes brackets are put round negative numbers for clarity only, and they may be ignored.

Examples

1. Calculate 3(-8 ÷ 2)
   = 3(-4)
   = -12
2. Work out (-6)^2 + 9
   = 36 + 9
   = 45

Exercise 2

Work out the following using your calculator:

1. 2 - 9
2. -4 + 13
3. -4 × -9
4. -12 ÷ 3
5. (-8)^2
6. 3(4 - 8)
7. (-7) × 3 + 2 × (-2)
8. $\frac{(-13) \times 2}{(-2)}$
9. (8-3) + 3(-5)
10. $\frac{5 - (-7)}{4}$

Rule for Addition and Subtraction

Replace +- and -+ with -, and replace -- and ++ with +, then proceed as if stepping up and down steps

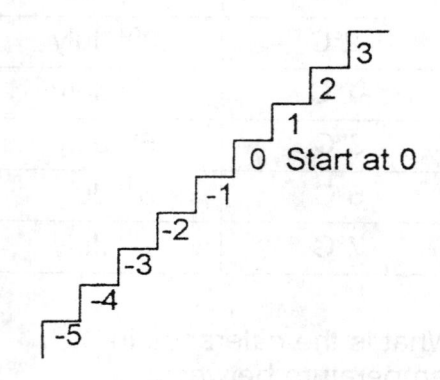

Examples

1. 5 + -7 = 5 - 7
   = up 5 and down 7
   = down 2
   = -2

2. 3 - 8 - (-4) = 3 - 8 + 4
   = up 3 down 8 up 4
   = down 1
   = - 1

Rule for Multiplication and Division

Multiply or divide the numbers as normal. If the signs are the same make the answer positive. If the signs are different make the answer negative.

Examples

-5 × 2 = -10   10 ÷ -2 = -5

3 × -4 = -12   -9 ÷ 3 = -3

-2 × -3 = 6   -6 ÷ -2 = 3

Exercise 3

1. -4 + -5
2. 13 + -5
3. 12 − -7
4. -6 − -2
5. (-7) − (-7)
6. (-9) − (+4)
7. -5 + 3 + 6
8. 2 − 7 − (-4)
9. (-6) × (-4)
10. 7(-5)
11. (-3) × 6
12. $(-4)^2$
13. 12 ÷ -4
14. -31 + 8
15. (-5) ÷ (-3)
16. $\frac{(-10) \div 5}{2}$
17. 3(-4 + 1)
18. 2(-4) + 3(-2)
19. Which of these are equal to zero?

    (a) -6 + 6
    (b) -6 − (-6)
    (c) 6 × (-6)
    (d) (-6) ÷ 0
    (e) 4(-3 + 5)
    (f) 2(-1) + 3(-4)

20. Work out

    (a) -3 + -8
    (b) 2 − (-6)
    (c) (-11) × 5
    (d) -15 ÷ -3
    (e) 4(-3 + 5)
    (f) 2(-1) + 3(-4)

21. For Canada the average temperature in January (the coldest month) is -10°C while the average temperature in July (the warmest month) is 31°C above this. State the average temperature in July in Canada.

14.4 Graphs and Charts

Axes and scales

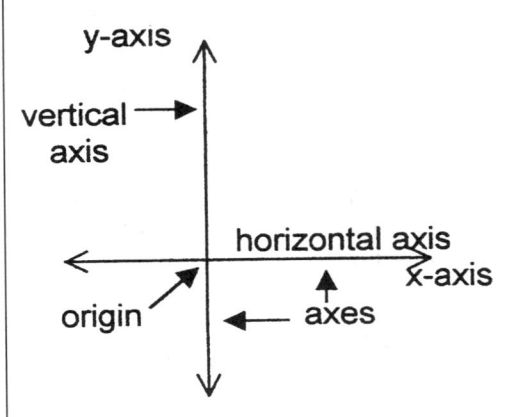

Graphs are used to show numerical information clearly. When drawing a graph you need to:

(a) choose a reasonable scale
(b) decide how to label the axes
(c) plot the points carefully
(d) decide whether the points should be joined with a straight or curved line
(e) join the points using a sharp pencil

The scale on the graph is the spacing between the labels on the axes. Number labels on the

147

axes should be spaced evenly, If you do not space the numbers evenly, then your graph will not show the information accurately. Try to fill the page without making your graph too big or too small. Don't forget to give your graph a heading

Example

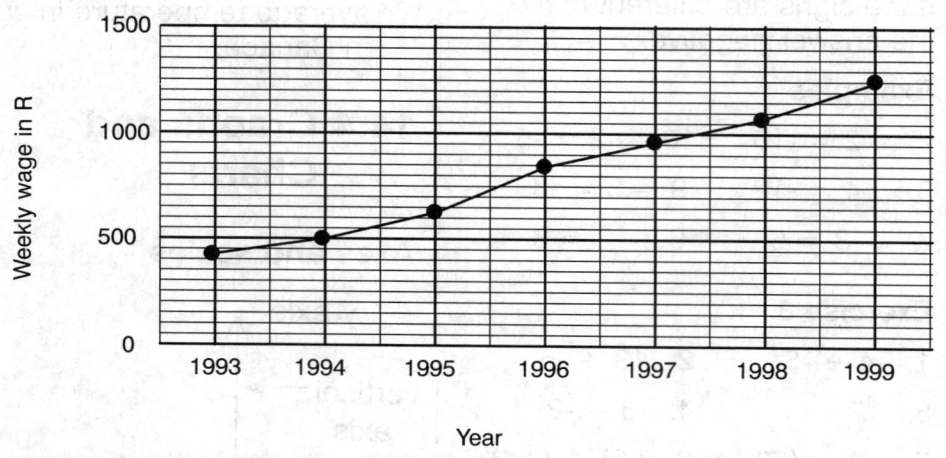

When drawing a graph, labelling the axes is essential. The units used should be clearly shown. The heading needs to be short but descriptive.

Coordinates

Coordinates show where things are on a graph or map

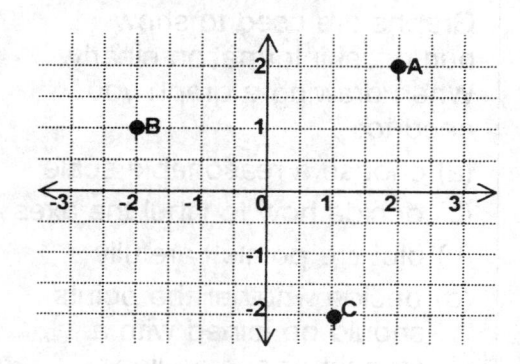

The coordinates of the point A are (2;2). This means that A has the 'address' of 2 units in the x direction (to the right of 0), and 2 units in the y direction (up 2 units from 0). B has the coordinates (-2;1) and C has the coordinates (1 ;-2).

A negative x value is to the left of 0 and a negative y value is down from 0.

Coordinates on a map are also written in a similar way, where a location is pinpointed by saying it is in the grid A2. Each square on the grid is labelled using a letter and a number. You looked at this in the unit on maps.

Plotting points

Graphs show a relationship between two sets of numbers.

148

Example:

A car was tested for petrol consumption at different speeds. The table below shows the speed in km/h and the fuel used (consumption) in km/l (kilometres per litre) at that speed.

The graph shows that as speed increases, so the amount of petrol increases, until you are travelling at 100km/h, and then the amount of petrol decreases as you go slightly faster.

Petrol consumption

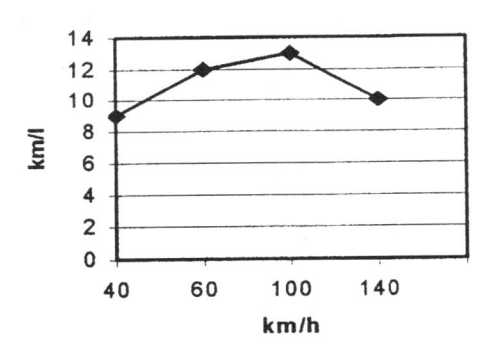

Exercise 1

1. Write down the coordinates of A, B, C, D and E on the graph below..

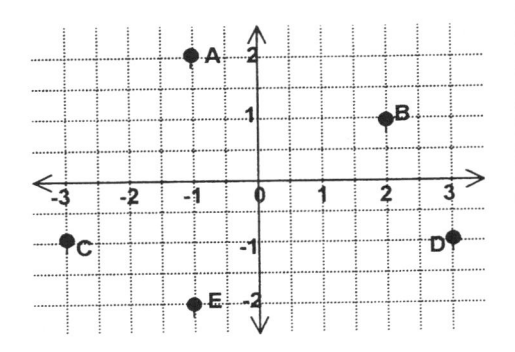

2. Using a scale of 1 cm per unit on both the x and y axes, plot the following points and then draw the graph using a sharp pencil. The graph should be a smooth curve. (-1;6), (0;1), (1;-2), (2;-3), (3;-2), (4;1) What would the value of y be when x has a value of 5?

3. The table shows the amount of American dollars the bank was giving in October 1999 for different amounts of rands:

Money in rands	60	90	210	240	330
Number of dollars	10	15	35	40	55

Plot these points on a graph. Say what scale you have chosen on the x and y axes. Join the points with a straight line. How many dollars would you get for

(a) R30 (b) R100
(c) R350 (d) R250

(e) How many rands would it cost you to buy $50?.

4. The graph on page 150 represents the journeys of a fast train and a stopping train.

Graph of train journeys

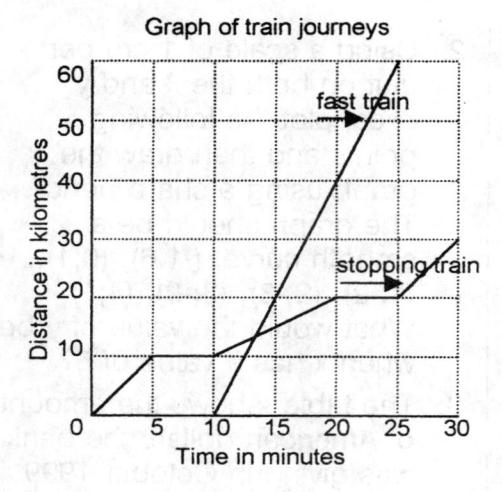

(a) What is the distance when the fast train passes the stopping train?
(b) How long does the stopping train wait at each station?
(c) Give the distance that the fast train travels in the first ten minutes of its journey.
(d) What is the average speed of the fast train?

Bar charts & pie charts

Bar charts

Some points to remember when drawing bar charts:
1. Use a sharp pencil.
2. Choose a good scale.
3. Draw and label the axes in pencil.
4. Make sure the bars are equal in width.
5. Draw the bars in pencil.
6. Write the heading and labels in ink when you have finished the graph.

Example

The exam results of 45 learners are given in the table:

Mark	0-20	21-40	41-60	61-80	81-100
Number of learners	5	10	10	15	5

These results are shown on the bar graph that follows:

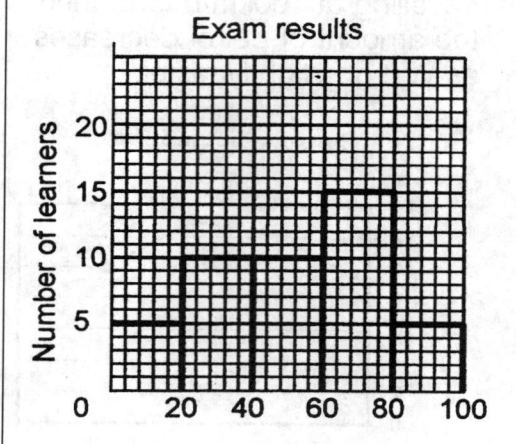

Exam results

Pie charts

Some points to remember when drawing pie charts:
1. Use a sharp pencil.
2. Draw a big enough circle.
3. Calculate the angles to the nearest degree and show your working.
4. Check the angles add up to 360°, allowing for rounding errors.
5. Label the sector of the pie chart in ink.
6. Work out the percentage of the pie for each sector and show it on the pie.

Example

Out of a sample of 300 people seen at the beach one Sunday, 65 were adults, 125 were boys and 110 were girls. Show this on a pie chart.

Total number of people = 300.

In the pie chart 360° represents 300 people.

So:

Adults: $\frac{65}{300} \times 360° = 78°$

Percent = $\frac{78}{360} \times \frac{100}{1} = 22\%$

Girls: $\frac{110}{300} \times 360° = 132°$

Percent = $\frac{132}{360} \times \frac{100}{1} = 37\%$

Boys: $\frac{125}{300} \times 360° = 150°$

Percent = $\frac{150}{360} \times \frac{100}{1} = 41\%$

Total degrees
   = 78° + 132° + 150°
   = 360°

People at the beach

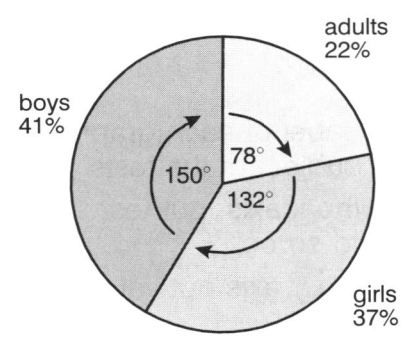

Exercise 2

1. A survey of where cars were made was carried out in a shopping centre car park. The results are shown on the bar graph.

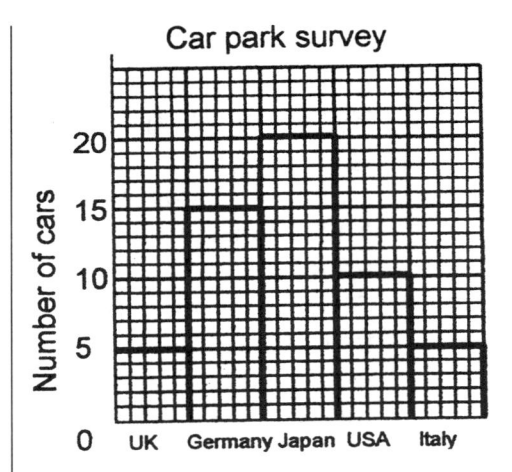

Car park survey

(a) How many cars were made in Germany?

(b) In which country were the most cars made?

(c) How many cars were there altogether?

2. The bar chart shows how many trainees, unskilled, skilled and managerial staff there are who work at the Hyperama.

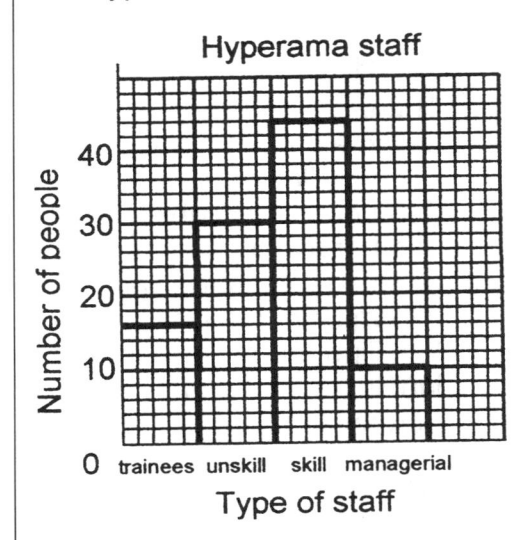

Hyperama staff

(a) How many skilled workers work at the Hyperama?

(b) How many people are employed at the Hyperama altogether?

(c) Give the number of managerial staff as a fraction of the total number of employees.

(d) Give the number of trainees and unskilled workers as a fraction of the total number of employees.

(e) Give the number of skilled workers as a percentage of the number of employees.

(f) Eight of the skilled workers are promoted and become managers. Four trainees leave and twelve new unskilled workers are recruited. Draw a second bar chart to show the people now employed at the Hyperama.

3. There are 15 000 people who live in a certain area. 2500 use candles on a daily basis, 3500 have gas lights, 750 use paraffin lamps, and the rest use electricity. Show this information in a pie chart, labelling the sectors with labels, angles and percentages.

4. Look at the pie chart showing the use of land

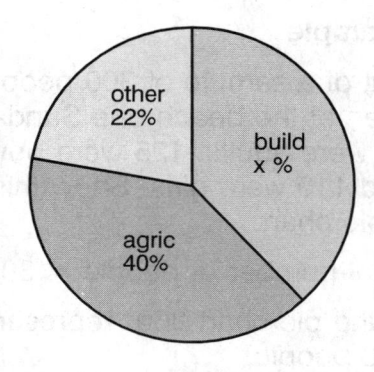

(a) What percentage of land is used for building?

(b) Work out the angle of the pie chart for other, agricultural and building using the percent and 360°.

5. Draw separate bar graphs to show the marks that you get in your class tests for all your subjects. Leave enough space on the bar graphs so that you can add to them as you keep writing tests. This will give you a good idea of your improvement throughout the year.

Hints:

(a) The label of each graph is the subject of the tests.

(b) On the x axis, put test 1, test 2 and so on.

(c) On the y axis put values from 0 to 100.

(d) Before you draw the bar for each test, make sure that the mark is out of 100 (a percent).

(e) You should have as many graphs as subjects that you do.

152

UNIT 15

Basic Algebra

Algebra is the name given to one of the many sections of Mathematics. It was first used by the Arab mathematician Alkarismi in the ninth century. Algebra was developed by Hindu and Moslem mathematicians.

Class Activity: Answer the following puzzle:

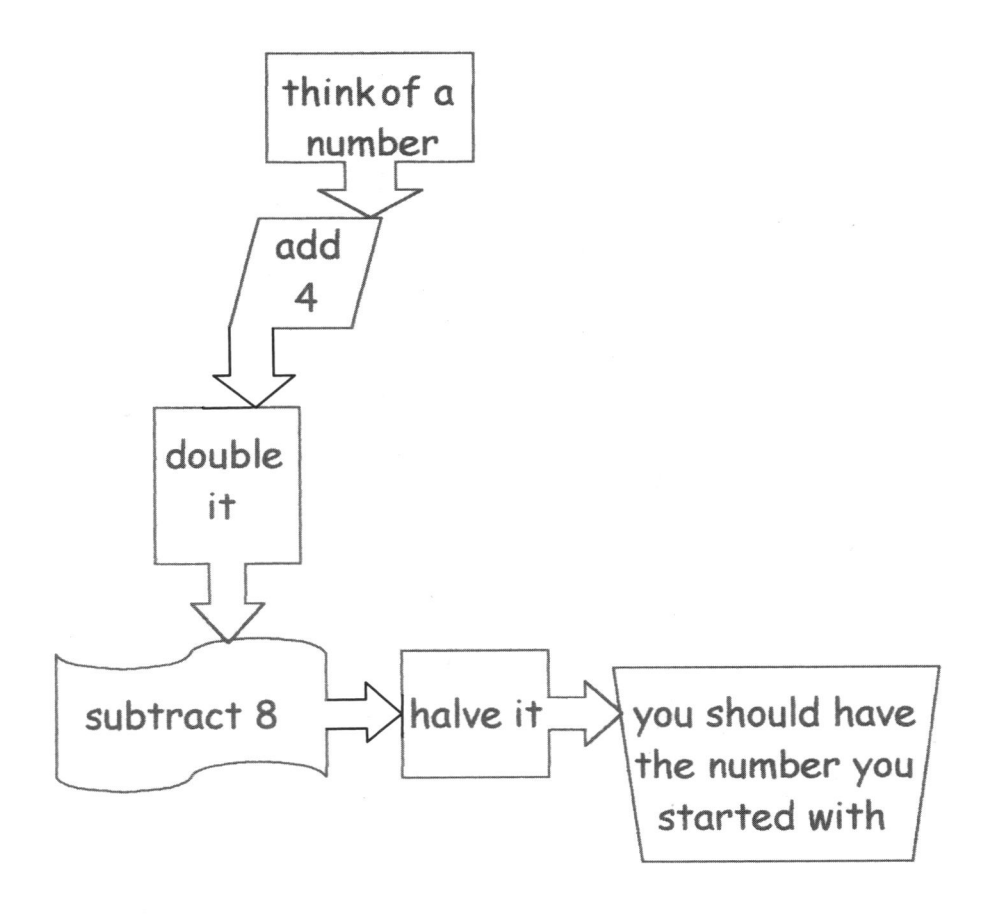

think of a number → add 4 → double it → subtract 8 → halve it → you should have the number you started with

The following table shows how you got to your answer:

	If you chose *1*:	If you chose *4*:	if you chose *7*:
1. The number:	1	4	7
2. Add 4:	1 + 4	4 + 4	7 + 4
3. Double it:	2(1 + 4)	2(4 + 4)	2(7 + 4)
4. Subtract 8:	2(1 + 4) − 8	2(4 + 4) − 8	2(7 + 4) − 8
5. Halve it:	$\frac{2(1 + 4) - 8}{2}$	$\frac{2(4 + 4) - 8}{2}$	$\frac{2(7 + 4) - 8}{2}$
6. The answer:	1	4	7

Each learner chose a different number, so the number can vary. When we use a letter of the alphabet instead of a number it is called a *variable*.

We can use the letter n instead of the numbers.
We just replace the numbers in italics with the letter n:

	If you chose n:
1. The number:	n
2. Add 4:	$n + 4$
3. Double it:	$2(n + 4)$
4. Subtract 8:	$2(n + 4) - 8$
5. Halve it:	$\frac{2(n + 4) - 8}{2}$
6. The answer:	n

We must be able to do the sums in row 5 of each table using the correct order of operations (BODMAS).

If you chose 1: $\frac{2(1 + 4) - 8}{2} = \frac{2 + 8 - 8}{2} = \frac{2}{2} = 1$

If you chose 4: $\frac{2(4 + 4) - 8}{2} = \frac{8 + 8 - 8}{2} = \frac{8}{2} = 2$

If you chose 7: $\frac{2(7 + 4) - 8}{2} = \frac{14 + 8 - 8}{2} = \frac{14}{2} = 7$

If you chose n: $\frac{2(n + 4) - 8}{2} = \frac{2n + 8 - 8}{2} = \frac{2n}{2} = n$

We use a letter (variable) when we want to represent something in a mathematical sentence and we don't know the exact number that we are starting with.

The variables that are most often used are x and y, but any letter can be used.

Using letters to represent numbers

Jeff, Balan, Thenjie and Mary help to clean up the fields near the school. Lots of bottles have been dumped there. They have a competition to see who can collect the most bottles. The drawing shows the number of bottles collected.

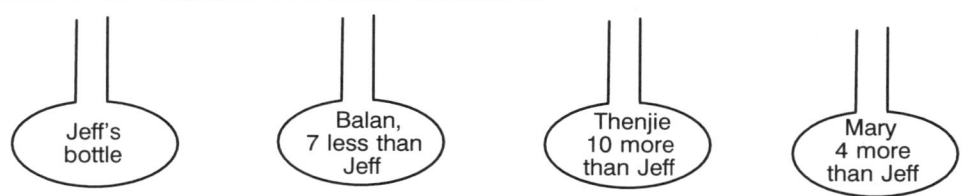

- Jeff's bottle
- Balan, 7 less than Jeff
- Thenjie 10 more than Jeff
- Mary 4 more than Jeff

If we let j stand for the number of bottles in Jeff's bag, then we can write all this information as follows:

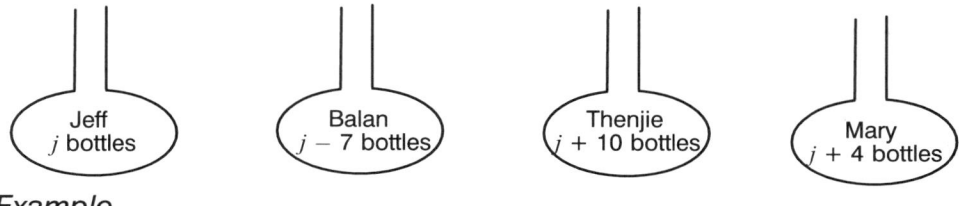

- Jeff j bottles
- Balan $j - 7$ bottles
- Thenjie $j + 10$ bottles
- Mary $j + 4$ bottles

Example

In a Maths test, Susan scored p marks. Write each of these people's marks using p.

(a) Wendy, who scored 6 more marks than Susan.

(b) Errol, who scored 5 marks less than Susan.

Solution:

(a) Wendy scored $p + 6$ marks.

(b) Errol scored $p - 5$ marks.

1. In a Science test, Hitesh scored y marks. Write each of these people's marks using y.
   - (a) John, who scored 21 less marks than Hitesh.
   - (b) Tom, who scored 11 more marks than Hitesh.
   - (c) Dick, who scored 1 less mark than Hitesh.
   - (d) Harry, who scored 5 less marks than Hitesh.

2. Sharon has x plants in her garden. Write each of these people's number of plants using x.
   - (a) Wendy, who has 7 more plants than Sharon.
   - (b) Kimberly, who has 13 more plants than Sharon.
   - (c) Nadia, who has 7 less plants than Sharon.
   - (d) Shelly, who has 13 less plants than Sharon.

The following week, the following number of bottles are collected by Jeff, Balan, Thenjie and Mary:

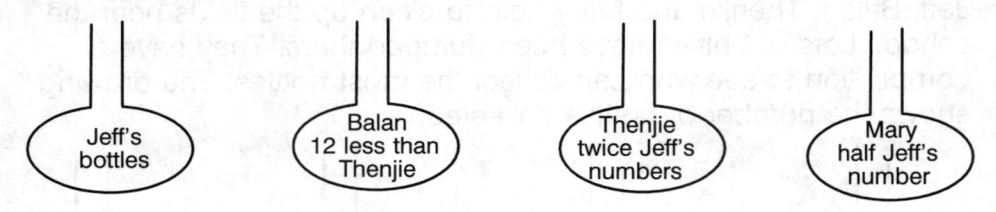

- Jeff's bottles
- Balan: 12 less than Thenjie
- Thenjie: twice Jeff's numbers
- Mary: half Jeff's number

This information can be written more simply if we use j to represent the number of bottles collected by Jeff.

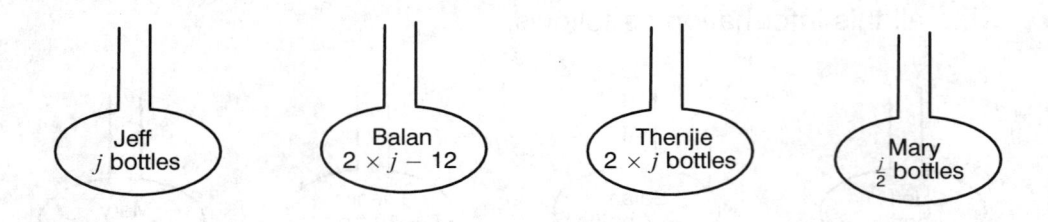

- Jeff: j bottles
- Balan: $2 \times j - 12$
- Thenjie: $2 \times j$ bottles
- Mary: $\frac{j}{2}$ bottles

In algebra we usually do not use the multiplication sign.

$2 \times r$ is written $2r$ (never as $r2$)

In algebra division is usually shown by putting one number over another.

$r \div 2$ is written as $\frac{r}{2}$

Examples
1. Sheila, Alan, Sally and Jonathan all collect stamps. Sheila has k stamps. Write each persons number of stamps using k.
   (a) Alan, who has 2 times as many stamps as Sheila.
   (b) Sally, who has Sheila's number of stamps divided by 5.
   (c) Jonathan, who has 20 less stamps than Alan.

Solution:
   (a) Alan has $2k$ stamps.
   (b) Sally has $\frac{k}{5}$ stamps.
   (c) Jonathan has $2k - 20$ stamps.

2. Write as simply as possible:
   (a) 4 times s
   (b) t divided by 7
   (c) 6 more than b
   (d) 12 less than z
   (e) 20 divided by h
   (f) v less than 8

Solution:
- (a) $4s$
- (b) $\frac{t}{7}$
- (c) $b + 6$
- (d) $z - 12$
- (e) $\frac{20}{h}$
- (f) $8 - v$

Exercise

1. Govan earns n rand each week. Write what each of these people earn each week using n
   - (a) Janet who earns 3 times as much as Govan.
   - (b) Ruth who earns half Govan's wage.
   - (c) Daphne who earns 25 rand a week more than Janet.
   - (d) Joe, who earns 15 rand less a week than Ruth.
   - (e) Kathy who earns 30 rand less than Janet.
   - (f) Chris who earns 12 rand more each week than Ruth.
   - (g) Ivan who earns 20 rand less each week than Chris.
   - (h) David who earns 45 rand more a week than Kathy.
2. Write as simply as possible:
   - (a) 3 more than e
   - (b) 18 less than v
   - (c) 5 times w
   - (d) w divided by 5
   - (e) 5 divided by w
   - (f) v less than 18
   - (g) 12 times d
   - (h) 13 more than y
   - (i) t divided by 2
   - (j) 2 divided by t
   - (k) 2 less than m
   - (l) m less than 2

Writing simple formulae (rules)

There are 12 pencils in a box.

How many pencils are there in:

(a) 2 boxes (b) 5 boxes (c) b boxes

Solution
(a) number of pencils = 12 × 2 = 24
(b) number of pencils = 12 × 5 = 60
(c) number of pencils = 12 × b = 12b

In other words we can write the rule:

the number of pencils = 12 × the number of boxes.

This is called a *formula* for working out the number of pencils in any number of boxes.

Let n represent the number of pencils and b represent the number of boxes. We can write the formula *in symbol form* like this:

$$n = 12b$$

Examples
1. A plumber is called out for a lot of emergencies. He charges a call out fee of R20 which he adds to the cost of any repairs he does. A formula for working out the plumber's total charge is:

   total charge (t) = cost of repairs (r) + R20

   (a) Work out the total charge if the cost of repairs is:
      (i) R50   (ii) R135
   (b) Write this formula in symbol form, using the letters in the brackets.

Solution
(a) (i) total charge = 50 + 20 = R70
    (ii) total charge = 135 + 20 = R155
(b) $t = r + 20$

2. Jane works in a supermarket. To work out her weekly wage she uses the formula:

   wages (w) = number (n) of hours worked × 5

   (a) Work out her weekly wage if she works:
      (i) 20 hours   (ii) 35 hours
   (b) Write this formula in symbol form, using the letters in the brackets.

Solution
(a) (i) wage = 20 × 5 = R100   (ii) wage = 35 × 5 = R175
(b) $w = 5n$

Exercise

1. When making a pot of tea for a group of people, Mr Mitchell uses the formula:

    number of tea bags (b) = number of people (p) + 1

    (a) Work out the number of tea bags used for:
    - (i) 2 people
    - (ii) 3 people
    - (iii) 4 people
    - (iv) 5 people

    (b) Write this formula in symbol form, using the letters in the brackets.

2. A baker works out the number of rolls needed to fill bags of two dozen rolls. He uses the formula:

    number of rolls (r) needed = number of bags (b) × 24

    (a) Work out the number of rolls needed to fill:
    - (i) 2 bags
    - (ii) 5 bags
    - (iii) 10 bags
    - (iv) 24 bags

    (b) Write this formula in symbol form, using the letters in the brackets.

3. A theatre has 500 seats. The manager works out the number of tickets left to sell using this formula:

    number (n) of tickets left to sell = 500 − number of tickets sold(s)

    (a) Work out the number of tickets left to sell if the manager has sold:
    - (i) 40 tickets
    - (ii) 100 tickets
    - (iii) 231 tickets
    - (iv) 449 tickets

    (b) Write this formula in symbol form, using the letters in the brackets.

Substituting values for letters

Examples

1. If $p = 15$, find the value of
    - (a) $p + 7$
    - (b) $p - 12$
    - (c) $20 - p$

Solution
- (a) $p + 7 = 15 + 7 = 22$
- (b) $p - 12 = 15 - 12 = 3$
- (c) $20 - p = 20 - 15 = 5$

2. If $z = 20$, find the value of
   (a) $2z$ (b) $2z + 5$
   (c) $\frac{z}{10}$ (d) $\frac{z}{5} - 2$

Solution
   (a) $2z = 2 \times 20 = 40$
   (b) $2z + 5 = 2 \times 20 + 5 = 40 + 5 = 45$
   (c) $\frac{z}{10} = \frac{20}{10} = 2$
   (d) $\frac{z}{5} - 2 = \frac{20}{5} - 2 = 4 - 2 = 2$

3. If $m = 5$ and $n = 8$, find the value of
   (a) $3m$ (b) mn (c) m^3
   (d) $3m^2n$ (e) $3m + 2n$

Solution
   (a) $3m = 3 \times 5 = 15$
   (b) $mn = 5 \times 8 = 40$
   (c) $m^3 = 5 \times 5 \times 5 = 125$
   (d) $3m^2n = 3 \times 5 \times 5 \times 8 = 600$
   (e) $3m + 2n = 3 \times 5 + 2 \times 8 = 15 + 16 = 31$

Exercise
1. If $y = 4$, find the value of:
   (a) $3y$ (b) $3y - 6$ (c) $\frac{y}{2}$
   (d) $\frac{y}{2} + 7$ (e) $\frac{5y}{10}$

2. If $m = 12$, find the value of:
   (a) $5m$ (b) $2m + 1$ (c) $\frac{m}{4}$
   (d) $\frac{m}{3} - 3$ (e) $\frac{5m}{6}$

3. If $p = 10$, find the value of:
   (a) $5p - 1$ (b) $5p + 1$ (c) $\frac{p}{5}$
   (d) $\frac{5}{p}$ (e) $\frac{p}{2} + 7$

4. If $x = 5$, $y = 6$ and $z = 3$, find the value of:
   (a) $3x + 2y$ (b) $2x + 3y$ (c) xz (d) $2xy$
   (e) $4yz$ (f) $\frac{10}{x}$ (g) $\frac{18}{yz}$ (h) $3x^2$
   (i) y^3 (j) z^4 (k) x^2y (l) xy^3
   (m) $2xz^3$

5. If $a = 4$, $b = 5$, and $c = 2$, find the value of:
   (a) $a + b$ (b) $2a + 3b$ (c) $5c - 2b$
   (d) abc (e) a^3b (f) a^2c^2
   (g) $17 + 2cb^2$ (h) $a(b + c)$ (l) $2ab^2c$

Simplification

An **expression** is when we have 2 or more 'things' added together or subtracted from one another. The 'things' are called *terms*.

$3x + 4y$ is an expression with 2 terms.

The terms are $3x$ and $4y$.

$2x^2 + 5x + 7$ is an expression with 3 terms.

The terms are $2x^2$; $5x$ and 7.

$2(x - 1)$ is an expression with 1 term. A bracket shows that the terms inside the bracket are treated as one thing.

$\frac{2x + 3}{4}$ is an expression with 1 term. A line is the same as a bracket.

$\frac{x}{2} + 3$ is an expression with 2 terms.

The terms are $\frac{x}{2}$ and 3.

How many terms are there in each of the following expressions:

1. $3x^2 + 5x + 4$
2. $6x^2y$
3. $6x^4 + 4x^3 - 2x^2 + 5$
4. $2(x + 3)$
5. $7(2x^2 + 3x + 1)$
6. $\frac{2x}{5} + 4$
7. $\frac{x + 1}{3}$
8. $x^2 - 2x$
9. $2x + \frac{x}{2} + 3$
10. $2x - 1$.

Write expressions for the following:

1. the sum of 7 and 5
2. the sum of 7 and x
3. the sum of x and y
4. the product of 8 and y
5. the number 5 less than a
6. the total of m and n
7. the number 3 more than x
8. the number n less than 10
9. the average of 2 and a
10. the number of times 2 will divide into y.

Write expressions for the following
11. (a) the sum of 5 and 7
    (b) the sum of 5 and y
    (c) the sum of x and y
12. (a) the product of 3 and 7
    (b) the product of a and 7
    (c) the product of a and b
13. (a) the difference between 8 and 3
    (b) the difference between 8 and p
    (c) the difference between q and p
14. (a) the average of 8 and 12
    (b) the average of 8 and x
    (c) the average of w and x
15. (a) the cost of 5 books at 75c each
    (b) the cost of a books at 75c each
    (c) the cost of a books at b cents each
16. (a) divide 30 cm into 5 equal lengths
    (b) divide 30 cm into t equal lengths
    (c) divide A cm in to t equal lengths
17. (a) If Steve is 15 years old, how old will he be in 6 years?
    (b) How old will Steve be in y years?
18. (a) If a car travels at 60 km/h for 3 hours, how far does it travel?
    (b) If the same car travels for h hours, how far does it travel?
19. (a) If three lengths of rope, each 2 m long, are cut from a piece of rope 10 m long, what length is left?
    (b) If two lengths of rope, each x m long, are cut from a piece of rope X m long, what length is left?
20. (a) A Student buys x books and y pens. If each book costs 85c and each pen costs 63c, what is the total cost?
    (b) If the books cost C cents and the pens D cents, what is the total cost?
21. Mr Smith is y years old; his son is 22 years younger. How old is his son? How old will the son be in x years' time?
22. (a) If I travel x km in 2 hours, and then y km in the next 3 hours, how far have I travelled all together?
    (b) What is my average speed for the whole journey?

23. Bob and Tom have R1 between them. If Bob has x cents how much has Tom?

24. (a) What is the next even number after 6?
    (b) What is the next even number after y, if y is an even number?
    (c) What is the largest odd number less than y?

25. (a) Two angles of a triangle are 25° and 79°. What is the size of the third angle?
    (b) Two angles of a triangle are $a°$ and $b°$. What is the size of the third angle?

26. (a) How far will a person walk at m km/h in h hours?
    (b) What is the average speed of a car which travels k km in h hours?
    (c) How long would it take to travel k km at m km/h?

27. (a) A TV set is bought for RP. If it is sold for RQ, what is the profit?
    (b) If a gain of RG is to be made what should the selling price of the TV be?

The **terms** of an algebraic expression are the parts separated by a + or − sign. A particular term is usually identified by the letter or combination of letters involved.

For example, in the expression $2a - 3xy + 6$, the terms are $2a$, $-3xy$ and 6; they might be identified individually as 'the term in a', 'the xy term' and 'the number term' respectively.

Like terms contain the same letter or combination of letters. Thus $2xy$ and $5xy$ are like terms, whereas $2xy$ and $3x$ are unlike terms.

An expression can be simplified when it contains two or more like terms, as these terms can be combined.

For example, $2x + 5x$ means '2 lots of x' plus '5 lots of x'

so $\qquad 2x + 5x$ can be written simply as $7x$

In the same way, $5xy - 2xy$ can be simplified as $3xy$.

When simplifying algebraic expressions, remember that, as letters represent numbers, all the ordinary rules of arithmetic apply. Some of the important facts are as follows:

Brackets are dealt with first, then multiplication and division are done before addition and subtraction.

When directed numbers are multiplied or divided, two of the same sign give a positive result and two different signs give a negative result.

When a string of numbers is multiplied, the order does not matter, e.g. $2 \times x \times 3$ is the same as $2 \times 3 \times x$, which can be written as $6x$.

Simplify

Simplify $3x + 4y + x - 7y$

Solution

$3x + 4y + x - 7y = 4x - 3y$

1. Simplify
   (a) $2x + 3 + 2 + 5x$
   (b) $3a - 2 + 4a + 6$
   (c) $3x + 5y - 2x$
   (d) $5t - 8 - 2t + 3$
   (e) $4 - 5p - 2 - 3p$
   (f) $a - 4b + 3a$
2. Simplify
   (a) $6 - 2x - 4 - 3x$
   (b) $10 - 5y - 7y - 3$
   (c) $2x + y - z + 3x - 2y$
   (d) $-a + 2b - 3a$
   (e) $5s + t - 2s + 6$
   (f) $4p + q + r + 2q - r$

Brackets

When we have something in brackets, we use the *distributive law* to multiply the number outside the brackets with all the terms inside the brackets.

i.e. $4(x + 3)$
$= 4 \times x + 4 \times 3$
$= 4x + 12$

And:

$2(2x - 5)$
$= 2 \times 2x + 2 \times (-5)$
$= 4x - 10$.

1. Multiply out the brackets
   (a) $3(x - 3)$
   (b) $2(3x + 4)$
   (c) $2(3x - 2)$
2. Multiply out the brackets
   (a) $5(x - 1)$
   (b) $4(3 - x)$
   (c) $3(a - 2b)$

When we have an expression with 2 terms and the one term is in brackets, be careful to use your rules for negative numbers carefully.

Remember: plus × plus = plus   or
plus × minus = minus
minus × plus = minus
minus × minus = plus

+ × +	= +
+ × −	= −
− × +	= −
− × −	= +

Example 1:

$$2x - 3(4 - 5x)$$
$$= 2x - (3 \times 4) - (3 \times (-5x))$$
$$= 2x - 12 - (-15x)$$
$$= 2x - 12 + 15x$$
$$= 17x - 12$$

Example 2:

$$x - 2 - (5x - 4) = x - 2 - 1(5x - 4) \quad \text{[We don't write the 1]}$$
$$= x - 2 - (1 \times 5x) - (1 \times (-4))$$
$$= x - 2 - 5x - (-4)$$
$$= x - 2 - 5x + 4$$
$$= -4x + 2$$

1. Simplify
   (a) $5x + 4(5x + 3)$
   (b) $7 - 3(4 - x)$
   (c) $3p + 2(4 - 5p)$
   (d) $x - (2 - 3x)$
   (e) $8 + 3(a - 8)$

- (f) $b - (5 - b)$
- (g) $4(2 - t) + 2(t - 3)$
- (h) $3b - 4(2 - 5b)$
- (i) $3(4 - x) - 2(1 + 3x)$
- (j) $-2(x - 1) - 3(x + 1)$

2. Simplify
   - (a) $3x + x(2 + x)$
   - (b) $a(a + b) + b(a - b)$
   - (c) $x(x - 2) - x(2x - 4)$
   - (d) $a(b - c) - (ab + c)$
   - (e) $x^2 - 3x(4 - x)$
   - (f) $x^2(1 - x^2) - x(1 - x)$
   - (g) $x - x(1 - x)$
   - (h) $a(b - c) - b(a - c)$
   - (i) $x(x - 3) + 2(x - 3)$
   - (j) $4p(q + r) - 2p(q - r)$